The Strength of a Woman

Activating the 12 Dynamic Qualities
Every Woman Possesses

The Strength of a Woman

Linda McGinn, Editor

With special contributors including: Ruth Bell Graham • Georgia Settle
Annie Chapman • Lucinda Secrest McDowell • and more

BROADMAN
&HOLMAN
PUBLISHERS

Nashville, Tennessee

© Copyright 1993
BROADMAN & HOLMAN PUBLISHERS
All rights reserved
4253-53
ISBN: 0-8054-5353-9
Dewey Decimal Classification: 248.843
Subject Heading: WOMAN//CHRISTIAN LIFE
Library of Congress Card Catalog Number: 92-35746
PRINTED IN THE UNITED STATES OF AMERICA

Library of Congress Cataloging-in Publication Data
The strength of a woman: activating the 12 dynamic qualities every woman possesses / edited by Linda R. McGinn
    p. cm.
    includes bibliographical references.
    ISBN 0-8054-5353-9
    1. Christian leadership. 2. Women in Christianity. 3. Women—Prayer—books and devotions—Christianity. I. McGinn, Linda R., 1953-
BV652.1.I67 1993
248.8'43—dc20

92-35746
CIP

Dedicated to Jesus Christ,
who in His overwhelming love
chose women to be used by Him for His glory.

Only in Him can a woman's
fullest potential be realized.
May each woman who reads this book
experience the joy of that reality.

TABLE
OF CONTENTS

Introduction

The sun shone brightly through the kitchen window that Saturday morning as three young women sat around the table sipping coffee and chatting about the upcoming conference to be planned. In an attempt to target the needs of today's women, they expressed their individual concerns.

Sarah sighed as she spoke. "Coordinating the Sunday School program at our church is a big job. Setting goals, making curriculum choices, and finding committed volunteers is tough. I believe God called me to this job, but I know I could be more effective. I need some tips."

Emily nodded in agreement. "Meeting deadlines, overseeing staff relationships, and delegating work responsibilities at the office demand constant interaction with my coworkers. The opportunity to integrate my faith in the business world excites me. As a manager, I want to learn how to exemplify God's character in all my relationships. I need suggestions for some practical ways to do this daily."

"Two months ago," Amy remarked, "I left a professional position to stay home with my young children. It's a decision I'll never regret, but I had no idea how much work is involved in child-rearing. That's not to mention shopping, carpooling, and all the other jobs a mother does. I want to exemplify Christ in my life to my children, but I need help. I feel really responsible for leading them God's way."

You are a leader. Wherever God places you, He equips you to be an example to others. "At least sometime in your life, you will be the best example of a Christian someone will ever see," writes one author.

What are the qualities that make a woman a successful leader? How can she exemplify these qualities in her life? How can she influence others to be productive for Christ's kingdom?

Leadership is both a privilege and responsibility. This book was written to enable you to examine your role as a leader and equip you to fulfill the task joyfully. Researchers have identified twelve qualities most essential to successful leadership.

In a recent survey, hundreds of secular employers and business administrators were asked to identify the ten top dominant qualities found in the lives of successful leaders. Invariably the same ten to twelve qualities surfaced. The most fascinating aspect of the survey was that each quality was biblically based. Each can be found in the Bible as a quality God desires to see in His people. Each reflects the perfect character of God. The ability to make wise priority choices; to grasp God's perspective or "vision" for the future; to act with integrity; to motivate; to encourage; to maintain a hopeful outlook; to be cheerful, disciplined, and humble; and to be an effective communicator comprise the ten most often cited elements for successful leadership.

Each chapter of this book highlights one of these qualities. A Christian woman presently influencing her world for Christ shares her insights and experiences as she applies that leadership quality in her life. Seven devotional Scriptures and thoughts follow, giving you opportunity for personal reflection and application. With the hope that you can join other women in discovering God's wisdom for successful leadership, small-group discussion questions close each chapter.

You may want to use this book as part of your personal Bible study and prayer time. Begin your week on Sunday by reading the chapter essay on a leadership quality. On Monday, reread the first part of the chapter, then turn to the "Thoughts for Daily Meditation" section. There you'll find weekday devotionals. Use these inspirational thoughts to guide you as you reflect on ways you can develop that specific leadership trait in your walk with Christ. If you are not already memorizing Scripture, take this opportunity to memorize one or more of the Scripture verses each week.

Whether you are Sunday School teacher, committee chairman, wife, mother, business woman, or all of these, I hope that in the pages of this book you will find biblical directives for leading others according to God's design.

May God's wisdom and insight be yours as you seek to identify His qualities for effective leadership. Through the shared experiences of Christian women leaders, may you find God's opportunities to implement His truth as you lead others for His glory, honor, and praise.

I want to take a moment to express my thanks to Mary Wilken for writing the daily devotionals at the end of each chapter. They provide a wonderful way to internalize the leadership qualities we will study.

Mary Wilken

Mary Wilken, Precept Bible study leader, freelance writer, and weekly prayer group leader, is employed part time at a Christian book store. She worked as a feature writer for the International Conference for Itinerant Evangelists in 1983 and 1986. Her work has been published in *Decision* and the *Upper Room*. Her husband, Terry, is employed by the Billy Graham Evangelistic Association, and she is the mother of three sons.

CHAPTER 1

LEADERSHIP QUALITIES THAT COUNT

Linda McGinn

Linda R. McGinn is the author of *Growing Closer to God, Resource Guide for Women's Ministries, The Bible Answers Questions Children Ask,* and the Bible study series *Women in the Word.* Ms. McGinn is a graduate of Gordon College, Wenham, Massachusetts, with a B.A. in biblical and theological studies. She and her husband Samuel are parents to Ruth, John, and Sarah.

Sweeping blonde bangs from her forehead, Dottie fidgeted with a paper clip. Burned coffee sent its pungent odor through the executive office, now her own. *I forgot to turn off the machine,* she thought. Dottie bit her lip and assessed the week's events.

Edith, the long-time office manager, had called her on Monday to report she was ill and would not be at work that day. Tuesday she was in the hospital. The physician diagnosed advanced pneumonia. Now it was Friday and Edith was dead.

Numb with shock, Dottie stared at her new office. She was Edith's logical replacement and here she sat. Many times she'd wondered how it would feel to be in Edith's position, but she'd never considered it a real possibility. After all, Edith was well liked and efficient.

Father, she prayed silently, *there is nothing I desire more than to be Your witness each day in this position. What a difficult way to begin. We are all hurting. Please let Your heart of compassion and love shine through me. Teach me what it means to be a leader. Empower me to lead in a way that pleases You.*

Webster defines *leader* as "a person who leads; directing, commanding, or guiding head, as of a group or activity; a horse harnessed before all others

1

on the same hitch or as one of the two horses in the foremost span."

God has placed each of us in some position of leadership, whether at home, church, office, or organization. How effectively we fulfill that responsibility depends on one thing—how completely we draw on Jesus' resources and example for direction. Paul writes in Ephesians, "And God placed all things under his feet and appointed him to be head over everything for the church, which is his body, the fullness of him who fills everything in every way" (1:22-23).

Jesus Christ is the "guiding head" Webster speaks of. We lead effectively only to the degree that we follow Him. Our method of leadership is found in Webster's second definition—one of two horses in the foremost span. Jesus describes His blueprint for productive leadership in Matthew 11:28-30, "Come to me, all you who are weary and burdened, and I will give you rest. Take my yoke upon you and learn from me, for I am gentle and humble in heart, and you will find rest for your souls. For my yoke is easy and my burden is light."

The word picture Jesus paints in this passage is that of a mature, sturdy ox yoked to one young and untrained. The steps of the mature ox do not vary or falter. The animal moves forward, plowing a straight, clear furrow in the dirt. The hooves of the immature ox wander and stumble, but the yoke keeps him moving forward as the daily training steadies his steps. Jesus desires to lead us as the lead horse or mature ox, guiding our steps, strengthening our weakness.

In defining leadership there are four broad areas for effective ministry: *Servanthood, Divine Appointment, Imitating God's Character,* and *Relinquishment.* Incorporated in this chapter are many aspects of these fundamental areas essential to Christ-honoring leadership.

SERVANTHOOD

The *first* area is that of servanthood. A good Christian leader is always aware that she is first a servant under the guidance and authority of Jesus Christ.

Frank Damazio writes in his book, *The Making of a Leader,* that *nagiyd,* the Hebrew word for "leader," has servanthood as a base element. "*Nagiyd* has as its root the picture of a man under authority, one who is subject to a higher power and who fulfills the wishes of that power. That was the kind of ruler God wanted to give His people: a man who would listen to His will and execute it faithfully with divinely appointed authority."[1]

Pointing out that by serving first the Lord Jesus Christ we are enabled to reach out in service to others, John White adds, "A true leader serves. Serves *people*. Serves their best interests, and in so doing will not always be popular and may not always impress. But because true leaders are motivated by a loving concern rather than a desire for personal glory, they are willing to pay the price."[2]

DIVINE APPOINTMENT

The *second* aspect of effective Christian leadership is that of divine appointment, or an understanding of God's call.

Mary accompanied the choir for the church worship services for 10 years. She came to me one day weary and despondent. "Linda, I'm tired of the weekly responsibility of accompanying. I feel no joy in it. I believe God has something else for me. I'm really excited about the possibility of coordinating the church's outreach program. I can't do both. When I talked with the choir director, she insisted that I must continue playing. There is no one to replace me and she seemed really angry. I feel trapped. What should I do?"

Mary and I discussed the meaning of "God's calling" in our lives. God calls us first to a deeper walk with Him. Drawing close to Him then enables us to discover the unique work God has designed for our particular service. It is this perfect place of ministry for which He, in His sovereign judgment, prepares and equips us. This is our "calling" from God. Thus, we read Paul's words in Romans 11:29, "for God's gifts and his call are irrevocable," and see Paul's identification of his personal call, "Paul, a servant of Christ Jesus, called to be an apostle and set apart for the gospel of God" (Rom. 1:1).

How can we identify God's calling in our lives? J. Robert Clinton writes, "God develops a leader over a lifetime. That development is a function of the use of events and people to impress leadership lessons upon a leader, (processing) time, and leader response. Processing is central to the theory. Leaders can point to critical incidents in their lives where God taught them something very important."[3]

As we identify those critical incidents and God's teaching, we begin to see His hand leading us to God-ordained positions of leadership. In Mary's case it seemed God was moving her to a new leadership role. As she became more confident of God's direction in outreach ministry, she was able to discuss it with her choir director. Together, they prayed for the person God equipped to replace Mary. Soon another came forward and Mary resigned graciously.

When we seek to follow God's direction for leadership and ministry, He provides the necessary adjustments to make His will possible. His plans and purposes soon become our first desire and then He fulfills the desires of our hearts.

In Ephesians 4:1 Paul encourages, "I urge you to live a life worthy of the calling you have received." Peter says, "Therefore, my brothers, be all the more eager to make your calling and election sure" (2 Pet. 1:10). Our desire should be to listen for and obey God's specific call. We can enjoy the leadership role by knowing that we are fulfilling His will.

IMITATING GOD'S CHARACTER

The *third* aspect of effective leadership is that of imitating the character of God. We are taught that God's desire is for us to be "conformed to the likeness of his Son" (Rom. 8:29). As we become more intimately acquainted with Jesus, we reflect His image. Exemplifying God's character is our most effective tool for successful leadership.

J. Robert Clinton writes in *Making of a Leader* that "leadership is a dynamic process in which a man or woman with God-given capacity influences a specific group of God's people toward His purposes for that group."[4] Through His Holy Spirit's power, God gives individuals the capacity to implement His character traits and qualities, accomplishing His purposes.

It should be our highest aspiration to see His character communicated through us and to see God's plans realized in the life of every person we lead. Our role is defined in 2 Corinthians 4:7, "But we have this treasure in jars of clay to show that this all-surpassing power is from God and not from us." We are vessels of God's person desiring to reflect His character as Christian leaders.

RELINQUISHMENT

The *fourth* attribute of successful leadership is that of relinquishing. Developing godly characteristics is a gradual process of trusting God's power and ability rather than our own. By doing this, we relinquish our desires and plans to God's will. Striving for accomplishment through self-generated methods and programs only leaves us driven and defeated.

In the article "Perfection Can Drive You Crazy," Ellen Futtermen writes of Ellen Sue Stern's book, *The Indispensable Woman*, "We live in a culture that gives women the impression that there is a way to be perfect. A lot of women are making themselves crazy striving for perfection. They feel this inner pressure to do it all and be perfect at it all."

Trying to be "indispensable" is the mistake. She continues, "Men in this culture tend to identify with two major roles—breadwinner and, more recently, father. Women tend to identify with multiple roles such as mother, wife, friend, sister, shopper, organizer, self-esteem booster. With all those roles, we attach a whole lot of responsibilities and expectations."[5]

To be an effective leader we must depend on God to work in and through us as we draw upon His strength. We then can take Jesus' words as our own, "If a man [or woman] remains in me and I in him, he will bear much fruit; apart from me you can do nothing" (John 15:5). True leadership flows from an absolute trust in God to accomplish His purposes by His power through us.

THOUGHTS FOR DAILY MEDITATION

"What does the Lord your God ask of you but to fear the Lord your God, to walk in all his ways, to love him, to serve the Lord your God with all your heart and with all your soul" (Deut. 10:12).

Servant-leadership is motivated by love for God. That love is reflected in our wholehearted devotion. Each aspect of the commands in Deuteronomy is interrelated. Our fear of God stimulates obedience while our love for Him activates our service. The tangible proof of our love is seen when we fulfill the role He has sovereignly given us. In leadership that means loving and serving those we lead.

Jesus said He did not come to earth to be served but to serve and to give up His life. He desires the same from His disciples. Following Christ to the cross marks a true servant-leader. *The Amplified Bible* says in order to serve Him we "must . . . conform wholly to My example in living and, . . . dying." Though Jesus recognized the difficulty of the task, His will was set to accomplish the Father's purpose. He knew the cross was the very purpose for His life.

From the beginning God has planned for us to become like Jesus, replacing our sinful character with His righteousness. This is the sanctifying work of the Holy Spirit in every believer's life. Sanctification is a process of being molded into Christ's image. Trusting God as leaders means relinquishing to Him our desires, our independence, our expectations, and our strengths. As Jesus was completely committed to doing His Father's will, His Father's way, we, by the Holy Spirit's power, can follow in His footsteps.

DAY 1

"Speak, for your servant is listening" (1 Sam. 3:10).

Young Samuel was ready to do whatever the Lord directed. The first task of his ministry as prophet was to speak the hard truth of judgment to Eli. He overcame his fear and told everything the Lord had revealed. As a result he grew in stature and the Lord was with him. His listening ear and servant's heart established his leadership.

Are you listening for the Lord's direction? Is there anything you're not willing to do for Him?

Prayer: Dear Lord, forgive me for when I am too busy to listen. Help me be eager to hear Your voice and do Your will.

DAY 2

"I am the Lord's servant," Mary answered. "May it be to me as you have said" (Luke 1:38).

Mary's willing response to Gabriel's assignment reveals her wholehearted commitment to God. A virgin made pregnant by the Holy Spirit! Yet, she extolled the Lord, claiming His blessing and favor to have been given such a task. The reality of her role cost Mary everything. She truly belonged to God.

To whom do you belong? What is your response to God's sovereign assignments?

Prayer: Dear Lord, forgive me for resisting sovereign assignments You have designed for me. Help me to know Your power enables me to do anything You desire and I can act in grateful response to Your love.

DAY 3

"The Lord has sought out a man after his own heart and appointed him leader of his people" (1 Sam. 13:14).

After Saul foolishly disobeyed the Lord and lost his kingdom, God looked for someone to lead whose heart belonged to Him. David's qualification to succeed Saul was his heart, not his perfection. We know of his moral failure with Bathsheba, and God knew even beforehand. But the Lord chose David because his heart was committed to Him. He knew that David would be the leader that He needed to do His work. You, too, were chosen by God to bear eternal fruit for His kingdom (John 15:16).

What kind of fruit does your leadership produce? Are you foolish like Saul or wise like David? Does God have your heart?

Prayer: Father, may my heart be steadfast in loving You. Cause my leadership to produce fruit that glorifies You and reflects Your love.

DAY 4

"Before I formed you in the womb I knew you, before you were born I set you apart; I appointed you as a prophet to the nations" (Jer. 1:5).

These words to Jeremiah confirm God's sovereignty and our appointment to ministry. Before his conception, Jeremiah had been approved and chosen as a prophet. The Lord consecrated him for the work. Then He strengthened and affirmed him to overcome his fears and do it.

We are called and assigned (1 Cor. 7:17). We must be open to His direction in the place He has assigned to us.

Prayer: Heavenly Father, I want a heart to serve You just as Jeremiah did. Thank You for loving me. It's almost more than I can comprehend—that You, the everlasting One, have a plan for my life. Help me to walk in Your way.

Day 5

"Follow my example, as I follow the example of Christ" (1 Cor. 11:1).

By the power of the Holy Spirit that Paul, like the other apostles, was able to bear testimony to Christ. Their leadership, established by God, was proven by their dependence on the Holy Spirit which gave them the grace needed to display Christ's character and do His work.

Paul's zealous commitment to Christ gave him memorable confidence in leadership. He said that because he imitated Christ, others could pattern their lives after him. In everything Paul sought to please God and win people to salvation. He strove to do both, not counting the cost to himself.

Does the Holy Spirit's power accompany your testimony for Christ? Are others able to see His grace through your life?

Prayer: Gracious Lord, I want to be a better witness to your power and glory. Fill me with Your Holy Spirit so that others might see Jesus' power through me.

Day 6

"Because by one sacrifice he has made perfect forever those who are being made holy" (Heb. 10:14).

God's one great act of relinquishment, the giving of His Son for sin, accomplished more than we can comprehend. Relinquishment is a powerful act. Trusting God as leaders means relinquishing to Him our desire, our independence, our expectations, and our strengths. Jesus was completely committed to doing His Father's will, His Father's way.

We must follow His example. How? By giving up our personal desires and by seeking to do His will. We must acknowledge our dependence on Him, setting our hope in Him, and realize our only strength comes from Him. Completely trusting Christ to perfect us and make us holy while enabling us to lead others to do the same is our mandate.

Are there areas in your life you need to relinquish to the Lord? Are you totally surrendered to His plan for you?

Prayer: Father, help me to trust You completely and to let go of any desires that may hinder my dependence on You. I want to do Your will.

DAY 7

"As long as he sought the Lord, God gave him success" (2 Chron. 26:5).

Zechariah instructed sixteen-year-old Uzziah, king of Judah, in the things of God. As long as Uzziah yearned for the Lord and sought after Him, God made him prosper.

But after years of wise and thoughtful leadership, Uzziah became prideful and was no longer satisfied to be a mortal king. He no longer wanted to accept the Lord's sovereignty. He entered the temple to burn incense and when confronted by Azariah, the high priest, and his eighty associates, he lashed out at them in anger instead of repenting. God judged him by striking him with leprosy, and he was forced to live the rest of his life weak and alone.

Thus, seeking after God, desiring Him and trusting Him above all else is the only path to true success. How do you perceive success? Do you yearn for the Lord's direction in your life?

Prayer: Dear Father, guide me to recognize that success comes only from desiring You above all.

FOR FURTHER REFLECTION

1. Four Bible women most exemplify the broad areas of effective leadership explored in this chapter. The first is the widow of Zarephath. Read 1 Kings 17. List the qualities of servanthood seen in the widow's life as she responsibly cared for Elijah and her son.

a. Read the following passages and write phrases which describe the attitudes each of us should have as servants of Jesus Christ.

Deuteronomy 13:4; Matthew 20:26-28; Ephesians 6:7-8; Philippians 2:3-11; 1 Peter 4:10

b. Describe three attitudes of servanthood you most desire to integrate into your daily life. Explain one way you can begin to exemplify these attitudes.

2. Priscilla had a clear knowledge of God's call upon her life. Read Acts 18 and describe the events and experiences which clarified Priscilla's call.

a. What do you believe is God's specific call in your life today?

b. Describe the events and experiences God used to prepare you to fulfill this call. (If you are unsure of God's call, pray for God's direction as you obey His Word in Romans 12:1-2.)

3. The nameless woman often referred to as the "Proverbs 31 woman" emulated God's attributes in her daily work and family responsibilities. Read Proverbs 31 and list those qualities which reflect the character of God.

a. Which qualities listed above would you most like to possess as you develop qualities of godly leadership?

b. Explain three practical ways you can follow this woman's example as your daily tasks are performed this week.

4. Learning to relinquish her will to God's greater purpose was a lesson Esther learned and applied. Read Esther 3—7. What aspects of godly leadership do you recognize in Esther's life?

Identify the most difficult event in your life today. Pray and ask God for the ability to trust Him as Esther did, relinquishing your will to His. Pray for His peace "that passes all understanding" as you trust Him with this situation in your life.

5. In which of the four broad areas of leadership do you need the greatest growth? Ask the Lord Jesus to give you fresh insight into His Word and new ways to develop in this area. As you obey His Word, He will reveal Himself to you (John 14:21), enabling you to lead effectively for His glory.

NOTES

[1] Frank Damazio, *The Making of a Leader* (Portland: Bible Temple Publishing, 1988), 18.

[2] John White, *Excellence in Leadership* (Downers Grove: InterVarsity Press, 1986), 88.

[3] J. Robert Clinton, *Making of a Leader* (Colorado Springs: NavPress, 1988), 25.

[4] Ibid., 14.

[5] Ellen Futtermen, "Perfection Can Drive You Crazy," *Richmond Times-Dispatch*, Sunday, April 2, 1989.

The most important quality a successful leader possesses is the ability to identify and apply priorities. The priorities a woman chooses will affect every area of her leadership.

In her article, "New Choices for Women," syndicated columnist Georgie Anne Geyer quotes several women who responded to the question, "What one piece of advice would you give to a young woman today?"

"I think it's to take control of your life and to do what is comfortable for you," Jean Baretta, senior vice-president at the Harris Bank, said thoughtfully.

"Know who you are, try to learn that early and identify your strengths. Then stretch to be the best at whatever success equates for you," advised Rear Admiral Roberta Hazard.

Oprah Winfrey, Chicago television hostess and movie star, admonishes, "Learn to be yourself and not be dictated to by what other people think you should be."[1]

This generation has been called the "me" generation. We are urged to evaluate and select priorities based on personal gratification—how things affect "me." But Christians apply different standards to identifying priorities—God's Word.

God gives specific guidelines in the Bible for determining priorities. He created the universe and designed its order. He knows which priorities will bring optimum effectiveness as a woman lives and works within the framework He designed.

Thus every activity in your life reflects a priority because you have chosen to apply the precious commodity, time, to each endeavor. You have selected each as one worthy of the expenditure of your energy.

Do your priorities reflect God's will in your life? Jesus lived according to His priorities and was able to say at the end of His life, "I have brought you glory on earth by completing the work you gave me to do" (John 17:4). How do your priorities enhance the accomplishment of the work God has given you to do?

As you read Ruth Bell Graham's essay, "Establishing Christ-honoring Priorities," prayerfully reflect on your lifestyle and the priorities it reflects. Seek to change any areas where your priorities differ from God's pattern for your life.

—L. R. M.

CHAPTER 2

ESTABLISHING CHRIST-HONORING PRIORITIES

Ruth Bell Graham

Ruth Bell Graham is author of *Our Christmas Story, Sitting by My Laughing Fire, It's My Turn, Prodigals and Those Who Love Them,* and *Clouds Are the Dust of His Feet.* Wife of evangelist Billy Graham, she was born in China to medical missionaries Dr. and Mrs. L. Nelson Bell. Mrs. Graham is a graduate of Wheaton College. She and her family live in Montreat, North Carolina, and have five children: Gigi, Anne, Bunny, Franklin, and Ned.

Priorities for all practical purposes means first things first, then second . . . third . . . fourth . . .

The Scriptures treat a certain order in the sequence of things. Suppose God had created fish before He created an ocean for them to swim in. Or animals and humans before there was land on which they could live. All of life is made up of "what comes first," "what is most important."

A thesaurus might give alternative definitions of *priority*: "after the fact or the right of preceding another, precedence, order, preeminence, arrangement." It doesn't help much.

Most procedures in life have steps to follow. "First the stalk, then the head, then the full kernel in the head" (Mark 4:28). A builder starts with a plan, then lays the foundation. I would have planned the interior, decorated the house, and landscaped the lawn before the bulldozers arrived. At one time I made all my clothing. There are priorities here too. With missionary parents, funds for clothes, while adequate, were not plentiful.

So I taught myself to sew coats, suits, and dresses.

After deciding what I needed, I'd select a pattern. Then knowing exactly how much material was required, I'd purchase the fabric needed for each pattern. It's essential to follow the instructions on the sheet carefully—step by step. From cutting to mastering the sewing and steam pressing the seams as you proceeded, it was rather like putting a puzzle together. And the results were reward enough for the trouble.

Choosing how to order our priorities can be difficult. To the newborn, his own needs come first—hunger, comfort, the need for sleep and cuddling. Even the simple uncivilized savage has his own set priorities. Mere survival heads the list.

To the single Christian it may be one thing. For the married, quite another. Each individual—married, single, divorced, student, homemaker, job hunter, job holder—must decide and arrange his or her own priorities.

My life is not the usual one. These days—when I wake up to a desk piled high with unanswered letters, boxes, and baskets stacked with books to be sorted and sent elsewhere, closets that need cleaning, life getting shorter with so much to do and diminishing strength—I realize I must set my priorities carefully and that there is danger in unordered ones. To me, priorities should come in this order: (1) God; (2) family—husband and children; (3) oneself; and (4) ministry.

Rightly ordered priorities are a sign of maturity. For the true Christian who wants above all to please her Lord and Savior, Jesus Christ, the priorities are simple but not easy.

GOD

Our first priority in life is our relationship with God and nothing less.

Once on returning home from one of his many trips, my husband Bill brought the children a small puppet. It hung simply by strings from hooks supported by two nails on the end of a stick. In their eagerness to play with it, the children pitched in and had a ball. Soon they brought it to me, a mass of tangled strings. To repair it, I had to hang it up by the hook to a nail in the fireplace mantel and slowly, patiently, painstakingly untangle the strings. So long as we kept the little puppet connected firmly to its overhead support, we were able to untangle it.

We are not puppets, but there is an interesting similarity. As long as we are firmly attached by our overhead support, we can remain that which we were created to be without becoming tangled. If we choose to put God first as He instructed in the Scriptures, our lives, like the puppet secured to the overhead support, will remain untangled even though we are used to the limit by the master Puppeteer.

God is not only our Creator and Father; He is our reference point in both His written Word and His living Word, His Son and our Savior. In Him "we live and move and have our being." He is the beginning of life for us.

He is our Guide, Comforter, Corrector, Encourager, Companion. All through our lives on earth, He is our Father in heaven. He is all we ever lived for and had here on earth, or longed for and never knew. God will be in all our dreams . . . and more. That we should allow Him to be in our lives is vital.

I recall the time in my life when I would wake up around 4:00 a.m. and get up eagerly, looking forward to unbroken time with God and my Bible. They were times of pure joy.

I recall also the times of desert wanderings when I allowed myself to be sidetracked and preoccupied with lesser things. I felt like the puppet severed from my Source and hopelessly tangled.

God has revealed Himself to us through His names, through His creation, through His Word, and through His Son. There is a great little book, *The Names of God*, by Nathan Stone. It is a classic—written by a brilliant scholar yet simple enough for anyone to understand. As well as through His names, we see God through His creation. "For the invisible things of him from the creation of the world are clearly seen, being understood by the things that are made, even his eternal power and Godhead; so that they [i.e., the doubters] are without excuse" (Rom. 1:20, KJV).

We also have the Bible that tells us all we need to know of God. Included are His commands to us, His instructions, what He has done, and a glimpse of what He is doing and will do in the future.

To study God's Word, look for a desk—if not a desk a table, if not a table, a piece of plywood on sawhorses—in some corner where you can place your open Bible. If there is a lull in the day, grab a cup of coffee and go to your corner. A verse—or even a portion of a verse—will nourish you for days on end. I think you shouldn't take a Bible verse out of context to prove a doctrinal truth, but for devotional purposes it is all right.

Finally, it is in His Son Jesus that He is the most perfectly revealed. John 1:1-14 tell us more of this. "The Word [Jesus] became flesh and made his dwelling among us" (v. 14).

If we put God first, study His Word faithfully, asking His Holy Spirit to help us apply it accurately and practically in daily life, we will not be problem free, but we won't be confused or entangled.

Family: Husband and Children

Husbands and family come next. Occasionally we can be torn between two or more priorities here.

Bill was away a good deal when the children were small. When he came home, naturally he looked forward to our times together. After cooking supper, washing the dishes, seeing each child was bathed, prayed with, and tucked into bed, I would go to our bedroom to find Bill sound asleep. Later—much later—he expressed his frustration (and some irritation) at my putting the children before him.

I wondered why it never occurred to him to care for the children while I cleaned the kitchen. In that way all things would have been solved: the children would have had a father to pray and talk with them. I would have had a lighter load, and Bill and I would have been together before he fell asleep. Had the children been a bit older I could have simply said, "It's time for bed. Daddy has been away a long time and we just want to be together." My priorities would have been on target, and I could help them to order their own priorities correctly in later years.

Oneself

Life in America seems more frantic, more high-pressured, than in other parts of the world.

Miss Edith Spurling, the English missionary and hostess of the very British missionary home in Shanghai, once remarked how she enjoyed having the Southern Presbyterian missionaries gather under her roof. "They have such a good time together," she said.

They did. The missionaries among whom I grew up were highly trained, thoroughly qualified, and deeply committed. They worked hard. At the same time, they knew that one essential part of hard work was recreation.

It is important that we take time out for ourselves—for relaxation, for refreshment. Yet it's so easy to overdo our pleasure or self-indulgence. My daddy was remarkable. Every day he started with God. After daily hospital rounds in the evening he would read aloud to Mother and us children. After the kids went to bed, he devoted his time to Mother . . . playing Scrabble or chess. He always kept his priorities straight—never lost his sense of fun.

There have been times when I sat on the front porch gently rocking and enjoying the view across the valley and the mountains beyond. I felt guilty because I wasn't doing something. Like a bow always strung tightly, we lose our resilience. The missionaries and I know the importance of releasing the string periodically to allow it to rest.

You can't make a person relax. Each one has to choose to relax in his or her own way. My husband studies the great Book and reading is not necessarily his way of relaxing. He would prefer walking, swimming or, for years, playing nine holes of golf. I, who am on my feet a great deal each day, prefer to sit with a good book.

Elizabeth Goudge writes in her book, *A City of Bells*, "It is sometimes the necessary in life to do nothing, but so few people do it nicely."[2]

Even more than relaxation is refreshment. Relaxation is one thing. Refreshment is another. We need to drink frequently and at length from His fresh springs . . . time in the Scripture . . . time in fellowship with Him . . . time worshiping Him.

On vacation, to return relaxed, I take along four books: one for a conversational resource as an icebreaker with strangers; one for information; one for relaxation and entertainment; and one for spiritual renewal and refreshment. Memorizing Bible verses and hymns is a great source of inspiration, encouragement, and strength.

Blaise Pascal wrote, "The sole cause of man's unhappiness is that he does not know how to stay quietly in his room."[3] Meditation has become a lost art in today's push-and-shove life-style.

"Work" was to George MacDonald's eyes not always required of a person. "There is a thing as sacred idleness, the celebration of which is now fearfully neglected."[4]

MINISTRY

The next priority is ministry. In my case, family is my ministry. Some who have failed to balance the two wisely have found grief. The price is devastating. One godly woman who traveled continually with her preacher husband said in later life, "My children are in hell today because I was away from home all the time."

Yet another mother, feeling the burden of raising her brood of seven, refused to travel with her minister husband. One day he left her, their large prominent church, and their children. She and I have become fast friends over the years. The last time we visited she said she should have traveled with him some. Not wanting her to blame herself, I disagreed.

"No," she replied, "in a divorce, there are always two sides. If I had just given a little and taken an occasional trip, perhaps it would have been different."

Identifying and ordering priorities for ministry are each woman's choice. She must find the balance. I keep in my Bible my friend Elizabeth Strachan's formula for a happy Christian life. It also applies to ministry.

1. God loves me—just the way I am unconditionally. Even if I never change, He will go on loving me and He will love me unto perfection.

2. Because He loves, forgives, and accepts me as I am, I love (in the right way) and accept myself just the way I am—in the body He has given me—with my limitations and imperfections . . . because He can use them as a showcase for His grace and glory.

3. Because God loves me and forgives me and accepts me, I love and forgive and accept my neighbor. Who is my neighbor? Whoever is closest to me: my husband . . . my children . . . my father and mother . . . my sisters and brothers . . . my teachers, etc. I pray, "Lord, help me to see that person as you see them."

4. The best way to express love is in simple deeds of kindness.

To quote Saint Teresa, in light of ministry, "Although we do not have Christ with us (physically) we have our neighbor, who for the *ends of love* and service is just as good as the Lord Himself."

THOUGHTS FOR DAILY MEDITATION

The Pharisees were amazed at Jesus' teaching. But to test Him, one of their lawyers questioned Him:

"Teacher, which is the greatest commandment in the Law?"

Jesus replied, "'Love the Lord your God with all your heart and with all your soul and with all your mind.' This is the first and greatest commandment'" (Matt. 22:36-38).

The primary goal for every Christian is presented in the First Commandment. Everything else she does depends on her response. To love the Lord supremely is our highest calling. Without that foundation our ministry will be ineffective at best. Our love relationship with God must come first, even before our family. That relationship establishes and validates all else.

Perhaps one of the easiest and most detrimental things that may harm that relationship is our failure to be still before the Lord. Demands of leadership often clamor for our attention, causing us to forfeit time for ourselves. But we must guard our time alone with God, or we will soon be ineffective in ministry.

Random busyness is one of Satan's most efficient weapons. If we are ministering by God's grace, He provides the benefits, opportunities, and all we need for the task.

DAY 1

"Seek first his kingdom and his righteousness, and all these things will be given to you as well" (Matt. 6:33).

The Father knows everything about us, everything we need. Our priority should be to strive after His kingdom and His way in order to be right with our Father in heaven. Then we can claim His promise.

The psalmist says that the "one" thing he required was to dwell in the house of the Lord "all" of his days (Ps. 27:4). His affection was set correctly upon heavenly things and led him to resolute action. He sought the only thing we all need, the Lord's presence in our lives.

Are you seeking His kingdom and righteousness? Where is your affection set? Do you pray earnestly for His presence?

Prayer: Heavenly Father, thank You for Your direction for my life. Help me to learn to keep You uppermost in my every action and thought.

DAY 2

"I rejoice in following your statutes as one rejoices in great riches. I meditate on your precepts and consider your ways. I delight in your decrees; I will not neglect your word" (Ps. 119:14-16).

The path to life is marked out for every believer in God's Word. "To some men, meditation is a task, to the man of cleansed ways, it is a joy."[5]

We have great riches at our disposal, riches too often neglected in our busy lives. We need to delight ourselves in the Bible, knowing it is God's Word to and for us. There we learn that Christ reigns supreme (Col. 1:18). We can take great comfort in that fact. His resurrection established His preeminence. Now the church, His body, is ruled by His love.

Do you dig for treasure in the Scriptures? Are you looking to His Word for the path to your life? Does Christ rule your heart?

Prayer: Dear Heavenly Father, help me find the treasures You have stored up for me in Your Word. Guide me in my search.

DAY 3

"For this reason a man will leave his father and mother and be united to his wife, and they will become one flesh" (Gen. 2:24).

The marriage relationship, two united as one, is an earthly picture of a heavenly idea. Jesus and the Father are one. The church is the bride of Christ. Husband and wife united together represent this sacred mystery here on earth. Marriage is the ultimate human relationship. No wonder our enemy Satan works so hard to divide us.

Today he declares all-out war against Christian leaders in their marriages. But the Scripture says the gates of hell will not prevail against God's church. We then must be aware of the battle and do everything in our power to nurture, protect, and honor this holy union.

Does your marriage come before your ministry? Are you nurturing and protecting your relationship with your husband?

Prayer: Dear Lord God, thank You for the sacred vows of matrimony. Help me to protect and nurture my marriage, to love my husband and children.

DAY 4

"We will not hide them from their children; we will tell the next generation the praiseworthy deeds of the Lord, his power, and the wonders he has done. He decreed statutes for Jacob and established the law in Israel, which he commanded our forefathers to teach their children, so the next generation would know them, even the children yet to be born, and they in turn would tell their children. Then they would put their trust in God and would not forget his deeds but would keep his commands" (Ps. 78:4-7).

When society has right priorities, children are received as a reward, not with regret. They are a gift only God Himself can give. Even the unique trials that parents face can produce a valuable reward—a greater dependence on God to help them through the ordeal.

God specifically commanded His people to make known to their children His dealings with Israel. It was their sacred duty to pass the faith on to the next generation. God used their spoken testimony to propagate hope and obedience. If this oral tradition was so valued that God established a law to command it, we would be wise to heed it also.

Have you told your children of God's work in your life? Does your life speak to them of His love?

Prayer: Dear Father, thank you for children. Help me to love and cherish them and provide them with wise counsel and judgment. Let me be an example of faith in Your love.

DAY 5

"Look well to yourself (to your own personality) and to [your] teaching; persevere in these things—hold to them; for by so doing you will save both yourself and those who hear you" (1 Tim. 4:16, AMP).

Paul admonished Timothy not only to give himself wholeheartedly to his ministry, but to take care of himself as well. We are not to neglect ourselves. That demands a delicate balance in our self-centered society, but it is an important warning.

Jesus calls those who are overburdened to come to Him (Matt. 11:28). He promises to relieve and refresh them. The burden He gives is light and easy to bear. All we need to do is to come to Him with faith.

Are you feeling overburdened? Are you able to balance ministry and your own needs?

Prayer: Thank You, Lord Jesus, for being there for me when I need Your assurance. Thank You that You hear and know me, that You will lighten my burden and give me peace.

DAY 6

"All this is from God, who reconciled us to himself through Christ and gave us the ministry of reconciliation" (2 Cor. 5:18).

Jesus Christ reconciled us to God. As His disciples we have been given the ministry that by our words and deeds we might bring others into harmony with God. Because of Christ our sins are no longer held against us. The different forms our leadership and service take do not alter that message. He chose us and appointed us to go and bear fruit (John 15:16).

The dictionary defines *appointed* as "designated, determined by authority." It implies the actual equipping for the task. Knowing this should put an end to our self-effort and striving. Perhaps you've been resisting His appointment. Remember, He does the choosing. Remain in Him. Is your ministry objective clear? What does it mean to you to be chosen and appointed by God? Are you producing the right kind of fruit?

Prayer: Heavenly Father, thank You for planting me in the place of Your choice. Empower me by Your Spirit to bear the fruit You desire.

DAY 7

"Feed my lambs . . . Take care of my sheep . . . Feed my sheep" (John 21:15-17).

Our love for Christ is proven in our care for His sheep. The call of leadership is that of a shepherd. Christ is our example—the Good Shepherd who laid down His life for His flock. Caring for sheep can be difficult work, but our love for Christ motivates and enables us.

Discouragement, weariness, and exhaustion are not from God. If we minister by His grace, He provides all we need for the task. Instead of wearing out, we will become more like Him each day. That is the work of the Spirit. Even though we may become tired, we will not lose heart.

Are you feeding His sheep? If you get discouraged at times, have you searched for the cause through prayer?

Prayer: Lord Jesus, I hear Your commands. Help me to feed others with the truth of Your Word.

FOR FURTHER REFLECTION

1. Setting priorities consistent with biblical truth enables us to function within God's ordained plan for His creation. This in turn ensures our peak efficiency as we fulfill His purposes for our life. Read Deuteronomy 6:4-9 and Matthew 19:19. Identify and prioritize the four major areas of involvement in a woman's life.

a. How much time do you spend with God? Does your daily life reflect a love for God above all else? Read Revelation 2:2-5 and explain the meaning of the verse.

b. Read Proverbs 17:6; 1 Peter 3; Psalm 127:3 and write phrases which show the importance God places on your family life.

c. Read Psalm 139 and Jeremiah 31:3. Do you know and reflect the love of God by the way you care for your physical, mental, emotional, and spiritual health? Why or why not?

d. Are you reaching out in ministry to those who daily cross your path in need of Christ's touch? Read the following verses and then write a paragraph describing God's will for us in ministry.

> Luke 10:30-37; Ephesians 4:11-16; 1 Corinthians 12:12-27; John 17:23

2. Make a list of one week's daily activities. Beside each item note the amount of time spent pursuing this activity. Example:

> Meal preparation ....11/2 hours daily
> Daily devotions ....15 minutes
> Bridge (or hobby)..............4 hours

a. Order above activities according to time expended from greatest to least. Now evaluate. What changes do you feel you must make so that your time will better reflect your priorities?

b. Read the following passages and write a phrase explaining why our use of time is important to God.

> Romans 13:11-12; Ephesians 2:10

3. List three changes you desire to make to reflect a commitment to order your priorities according to God's Word and will in your life.

NOTES

[1]Georgie Anne Geyer, "New Choices for Women," *Richmond Times-Dispatch*, syndicated 1986, Universal Press Syndicate.

[2]Elizabeth Goudge, *A City of Bells* (Gerald Duckworth and Company, 1949), 291.

[3]Blaise Pascal, *Les Pensées* (Penquin Books, 1961), 205.

[4]George MacDonald, *Anthology,* Lewis, C. S.–Introduction (Great Britain: Robert MacLebose & Co., Ltd., 1970), 109.

[5]Charles H. Spurgeon, *The Treasury of David* (Grand Rapids, Mich.: Kregel Publications, 1986), 516.

Having considered the broad perspective of leadership and one of the elements—priorities—we now look at the second most desired quality for a Christian woman leader—vision.

Merrill J. Oster in his book, *Vision-Driven Leadership*, writes, "vision is a guiding light to live by 365 days a year. It is the reason you go to work and the reason your organization exists. A real vision gets tucked away in the mind, not the drawer; it shapes every thought and decision."[1]

To a Christian woman leader, Jesus Christ is that guiding light. "God is light; in him there is no darkness at all" (1 John 1:5). Desiring God's will and His "kingdom perspective" (acknowledging the present reality of God's kingdom where He is the reigning King) shapes our vision for daily direction and goals. We seek God's plans and purposes first. We learn how to help others accomplish these goals while maintaining the "big picture."

Oster continues, "A vision is a spiritual statement of one's relation to God and the rest of humanity. It is the very quality that makes it so relevant to our day-to-day experience; a true vision is a blueprint for daily action."[2]

The article, "I Do Firmly Resolve," suggests breaking up a resolution into small components and setting intermediate, easily attainable goals within a specific time period, moving in a positive direction toward an ultimate goal by taking small steps at first will increase the chances for success and is preferable in most cases to plunging right in or never making a move at all.[3]

Learning how to bring forth godly change as a leader excites and challenges. "Maintaining a Visionary Perspective" stresses the importance of vision to leadership and offers guidance for becoming a change agent in whatever setting God has placed you.

—L. R. M.

CHAPTER 3

Maintaining a Visionary Perspective

T. R. Hollingsworth & Gladys Israels

T.R. Hollingsworth is a writer, instructor, speaker, and editor. Adjunct instructor of creative writing at John Tyler Community College, she has edited Linda R. McGinn's books and contributed to *The Bible Answers Questions Children Ask.* Hollingsworth serves as regional advisor for the Mid-Atlantic Region of the Society of Children's Books Writers.

Two women work side-by-side, listening to the muted conversation of the twelve men gathered around the table, waiting for their meal. One slips away and crouches behind the men, listening to the talk.

Sometime later, the other woman rushes toward the group, complaining that she has been left to do all the work while her sister lounged leisurely among the men.

The speaker raises his hand and says, "Martha, Martha . . . you are worried and upset about many things, but only one thing is needed. Mary has chosen what is better, and it will not be taken away from her" (Luke 10:41-42).

Mary was a woman of vision. She was able to focus on the important event of the day. Perhaps, without realizing it, she recognized the significance of having the Lord in her home and anticipated the events to come.

In another incident, Jesus was in Bethany at the home of a Pharisee. Again, the men were gathered around the dinner table, eating and talking. One of the attending women, an acknowledged sinner, approached the Lord and, taking an expensive bottle of perfume, poured it over His head. Her tears wet His feet, and she wiped them away with her long, flowing hair. You can imagine the pungent odor that must have permeated the room.

The men at the table did not recognize her vision. But Jesus did. He told her, "Your sins are forgiven" (Luke 7:48). The others, still unaware that God dwelled among them, grumbled about the waste, thinking the expensive perfume could have been used to feed the poor or fill the disciples' treasury. Their vision was clouded; the woman instinctively knew her Lord and Savior. She had vision.

Many of us have met or worked with leaders who show a vision for their work, for the people they lead, for needed change, and for the future.

What common qualities are found in such leaders? Leroy Eims, in his book, *Be a Motivational Leader*, writes, "To maintain a high degree of motivation and morale, the leader must develop the people involved with him, helping them to reach their fullest potential."[4] To do this the qualities of honesty, loyalty, generosity, and humility are vital to a visionary leader.

We can look at Nehemiah to identify other qualities shown by godly visionaries. A wealthy man, Nehemiah sacrificed his own comfort to serve God and his people. His courage, his consistent personal example of commitment to godliness, and his unwavering truthfulness and fierce determination to accomplish his assigned work exemplify the traits of a leader with vision.

Like Nehemiah, a visionary leader strives to put the kingdom of God first in her thinking. She recognizes Christ's example for a "kingdom perspective" in the prayer He gave us, "Thy will be done on earth as it is in heaven" (Matt. 6:10). She asks, "What is God's heavenly will, the will of His kingdom to be accomplished here in this situation?"

Gladys Israels is executive assistant to Dr. James Kennedy of Evangelism Explosion III International. Her duties include coordinating Dr. Kennedy's involvement with EE, Coral Ridge Ministries, Knox Seminary, and the Coral Ridge Executive staff. Mrs. Israels is involved in the EE training ministry of Coral Ridge PCA Church, Fort Lauderdale, Florida. She and her husband Roger have one daughter, Kathy.

To seek first the kingdom of God is to acknowledge that God is the absolute sovereign Lord over our personal worship, our moral and ethical values, our personal relationships, and our service to others.

A visionary leader believes and accepts this truth. She believes God, expecting Him to supply insight while pouring out His grace and mercy. Like Nehemiah, the visionary leader opens her mind and heart to the Lord through prayer, seeks His guidance, then reaches out with faith and expectation of success.

John Calvin said it is the responsibility of the visible church to make the invisible things of the kingdom visible! Jesus Christ said, "Let your light shine before men, that they may see your good deeds and praise your Father in heaven" (Matt. 5:16).

The church has the responsibility of demonstrating to our unbelieving culture the invisible things of the kingdom—to show our world today that Jesus Christ reigns. Can you imagine what the church of Jesus Christ could accomplish? What would the kingdom of God in our day look like if every Christian prayerfully sought to maximize her potential under His lordship?

Charles Swindoll, in *Quest for Character,* says that vision is "spawned by faith, sustained by hope, sparked by imagination and strengthened by enthusiasm."[5]

VISION FOR LEADING

In his book, *Transforming Leadership,* Leighton Ford quotes Thomas Sowell's view of a person with vision. "Visions are the silent shapers of our thought."[6] A profound statement.

Are you an "idea person"? We've all known people who seem to come up with an original idea almost spontaneously. Whatever the situation, she envisions the complete picture, the possible problems, the solutions, and the final outcome.

Not all of us are "idea people." Even so, to be an effective leader of women, it's essential to have a vision for the task, for the women who follow your lead and for the outcome. In other words, before the first action is taken, the leader should envision the complete process.

To become a visionary leader, we can learn from others who have already developed that quality. Again, Leighton Ford writes, "Vision is the very stuff of leadership—the ability to see in a way that compels others to pay attention. . . . As a student once put it, 'Leaders point us in the right direction and tell us to get moving.' Vision is like a magnifying glass which creates focus, a bridge which takes us from the present to the future, a target that beckons."[7]

So, a visionary leader must be focused. In other words, she can see the many strokes that lead to the "big picture" while keeping the final product in mind. To present the details to those she leads, she must have initiative, courage, enthusiasm, and creative energy.

Paul knew the value of initiative and enthusiasm when he wrote to encourage the early Christians of Corinth. "For I know your eagerness to help, and I have been boasting about it to the Macedonians, telling them that since last year you in Achaia were ready to give; and your enthusiasm has stirred most of them to action" (2 Cor. 9:2).

Leaders who excel are creative. We need only look at the lives of the apostles. They weren't afraid to try a new way of thinking and living. They reached out to others with new thoughts and words—nothing boring or monotonous about them.

They knew that God is a God of variety, of order. They only needed to look at Jesus to see that—His message was new, His message was vital, His message was exciting. And they followed.

Eims writes in another book, *Be the Leader You Were Meant to Be:*

> How do you gain a creative spirit? One way is to keep yourself in the proper frame of mind. Constantly be on the lookout for a better way. Train yourself to think, "If it works, it will soon be obsolete." Maintain an open and probing mind. Pray for the boldness and courage it will take to try something new when God reveals it to you.[8]

VISION FOR COOPERATION

Knowing that the Holy Spirit will strengthen your leadership highlights the need for the cooperative effort of others. Without that, leadership would be useless. Who can be a visionary leader without followers?

Not all leaders have the cooperation of their followers. Have you watched to see why some leaders succeed and others fail? Have you noticed the qualities of the effective leader who holds the respect and co-operation of the ones she leads?

Visionary leaders don't look at the ones they lead as subordinates. They consider them as future leaders. They are in training for more responsibility. Those you lead should:

1. *Agree with your goals and objectives.* You must have acquainted them not only with the projected outcome but also the many tasks leading to it. With your encouragement, they should consider their assigned role important to the accomplishment of the goals and desire to cooperate to reach them.

2. *Be able to handle the responsibility assigned without an emotional reaction.* If you have seriously considered the qualities and abilities of those you lead, you will be careful to assign tasks that each can accomplish with pleasure and satisfaction.

3. *Help your coworkers develop a spirit of faithfulness, to be individuals you can count on to complete their work on time and satisfactorily.* Christian women leaders can look to Jesus for guidance in this. Jesus said, "Whoever can be trusted with very little can also be trusted with much" (Luke 16:10). This infers that by beginning with small jobs and trusting your helpers to perform them well and on time, you can then give them greater responsibilities. Thus, failures will be few and a spirit of faithfulness enhanced. You have helped each mature.

Vision for Change

Jesus was and is the original change agent. We need only look at His ministry to see that He kept before Him His Father's vision to purchase our salvation and always remained faithful to His will. "For I have come down from heaven not to do my will but to do the will of him who sent me" (John 6:38). Jesus brought a new life-style that was radically different from the religion of the Jews. Following Jesus required a completely new approach to life.

Visionary leaders are change agents for Christ. They, alone, know that true change can occur only through the Lord Jesus Christ.

How can you become a change agent for Jesus? First, you should go to the Lord in prayer. "Seek the Lord while he may be found; call on him while he is near" (Isa. 55:6). Then look at your own life.

Is there something in your life that needs changing—a tense relationship, a troubled family life, a personality problem or conflict? By becoming the woman that the Lord wants you to be, you can trust Him to help you solve the deep personal issues, equipping you to reach out effectively to others.

Then look at your local church. It's often said that one person can make a difference, and I know it to be a truth. When my son was in elementary school, a notice was sent to parents that there would be a sex education planning meeting. A film would be shown to describe the program planned for the fifth and sixth graders. When I arrived in the school, I found that only a few parents had bothered to interrupt their day for the meeting.

I was shocked by the film, for it left little to the imagination. The meeting was opened for discussion. Again, I was shocked. The parents were not only supportive; they were encouraging.

Finally, I stood. I simply said, "I'd like to know when you plan to show this film so I can keep my son out of school that day." Immediately a man stood, identified himself as a family physician, and gave detailed description of the harm he thought the film might cause. The program was canceled.

VISION FOR THE FUTURE

In their book, *Megatrends 2000,* John Naisbitt and Patricia Aburdene dedicate a chapter to the religious revival to come. They write that throughout history, the turn of a century often heralded a religious reformation.

> For within the symbolism of the millennium is the apocalyptic battle between good and evil. Will we face the demise of civilization as we know it by nuclear accident or the greenhouse effect? . . . The millennium is a two-sided metaphor of choice. On the one side, a man-made apocalypse represents the possibility that godlike technology in human hands could destroy the environment.[9]

Naisbitt and Aburdene predict that at the turn of the century, a choice will be made between the pursuit of good or evil. Finally, they write, "As the symbolic year 2000 approaches, humanity is not abandoning science, but through this religious revival, we are reaffirming the spiritual in what is now a more balanced quest to better our lives and those of our neighbors."[10]

As Christian leaders, we can dismiss this as a secular viewpoint and go on our merry way. Or we may be challenged by it and consider how we will be part of the changing world in the year 2000.

To become an agent for change, first we must have a plan. A plan demands goals. What are your goals for change?

John White in his book, *Excellence in Leadership*, says that goals:

➤ give a sense of direction.
➤ give us power to live in the present.
➤ promote enthusiasm and strong organizational life.
➤ help us to operate effectively.
➤ help us evaluate progress.
➤ force us to plan ahead.
➤ help us communicate within organization.
➤ give people clear understanding of what is expected.
➤ help to reduce needless conflict and duplication.
➤ take emphasis *off* activity and place it *on* output.[11]

Before setting your goals for change, pray for God's guidance and support. Decide on your specific purposes. What do you want to change? Are there obstacles to be overcome? What are your plans to do this?

With the help of your coworkers, develop your plan, design your goals, and delegate and assign duties and activities.

Then take that final step and launch your effort. Trust the Lord to see you through the difficulties, roadblocks, and negative influences. You're on your way to join the other change agents that the Lord has selected to spread His Word.

THOUGHTS FOR DAILY MEDITATION

"Where there is no vision, the people perish" (Prov. 29:18, KJV).

Vision compels leaders to lead and followers to follow. Vision is a way of serving—a perspective on the reality of God in our lives. As this verse in Proverbs explains, people need vision.

A successful leader uses her way of seeing to inspire those she leads. All godly people in both the Old and New Testaments had an unshakable vision of God and His call on their lives. That vision saw them through the trials and testings of their faith. It held them securely to the right road, no matter what the circumstances. It made them a model to follow.

Seeing God and His kingdom through the eyes of faith is essential to Christian leadership. Passing on that godly perspective to others is a vital task of leading.

DAY 1

"So we fix our eyes not on what is seen, but on what is unseen. For what is seen is temporary, but what is unseen is eternal" (2 Cor. 4:18).

As leaders our focus, our vision, and our faith are set on invisible realities. By the world's standard, reality is determined by what is seen. But spiritual reality relies on heavenly perspective to understand real truth. That truth is everlasting. What the world sees is brief and fleeting.

We not only *have* faith; we conduct our lives by its conviction. Faith affects our thinking and our doing. We regulate our actions by our belief regarding divine things. Therefore, we do not walk by what we see.

Does your faith determine your conduct? Is the reality of your life determined by the seen or unseen?

Prayer: Gracious Father, You know that at times I am influenced by the realities of the world. Help me seek spiritual reality and Your truth.

DAY 2

"'No eye has seen, no ear has heard, no mind has conceived what God has prepared for those who love him'—but God had revealed it to us by his Spirit" (1 Cor. 2:9).

The Holy Spirit is given to believers that we might realize and comprehend the gifts God so lavishly gives us. Before Jesus' resurrection, these things were hidden. But now the Spirit of God reveals them to us! With that vision, we can lead others to obedience so they can gratefully recognize and hope for His benefits.

Do you rely on the Spirit's perspective for your insight? Are you leading others to understand His benefits?

Prayer: Heavenly Father, thank You for the gifts You have given me, so many that I can hardly count them. Help me to use them with vision as I strive to lead others.

DAY 3

"So may all your enemies perish, O Lord! But may they who love you be like the sun when it rises in its strength" (Judg. 5:31).

The Bible relates many stories of leaders with vision. Their faith and perspective inspired the people to follow God through difficult and prosperous times. Their vision was the impetus for action that led God's people to victory and restoration.

The Israelites were oppressed for twenty years by Sisera, the powerful general of the army of Canaan. During this time Deborah was leading Israel as their judge. She was the only judge who was also a prophetess. Through her, the Lord commanded the Israelite army to rise up against Sisera.

Deborah even agreed to go to the battle with the army when they lacked the courage to face the enemy. At her command the evil army was routed and all their troops killed. Because of her courageous leadership and vision, she was able to deliver her people from oppression and save the promised land. Israel then had peace for forty years.

How does your vision of God's power over His enemies inspire your courage in leading? Do you encourage others to look to Him for victory?

Prayer: Father, we want to be women of vision, compelling others to faith and righteous deeds. Inspire us to see You as You really are through the lives and actions of women of vision who loved and followed You.

DAY 4

"She never left the temple but worshiped night and day, fasting and praying" (Luke 2:37).

Anna was a visionary with a heart for her God. As a prophetess she faithfully waited for the Lord to fulfill His promise to Israel and send the Messiah. For eighty-four years she worshipped and prayed in the temple. When Joseph and Mary brought Baby Jesus to Jerusalem for the customary purification, Anna saw Him and gave thanks to God. She spoke of Jesus to all who were looking for the redemption.

Are you a patient believer as you wait for God's promises to be fulfilled? Do you persevere in prayer and worship as you wait?

Prayer: Heavenly Father, I praise Your Holy Name and thank You for Your promises. Help me to be a patient believer.

Day 5

"By faith he made his home in the promised land like a stranger in a foreign country; he lived in tents, as did Isaac and Jacob, who were heirs with him of the same promise. For he was looking forward to the city with foundations, whose architect and builder is God" (Heb. 11:9-10).

Biblical visionaries of old, like Abraham, Caleb, and David, still inspire us as we look with hope to our future. Having vision and perseverance is the mark of all good leaders.

Abraham went to live in a foreign country without even knowing where he was going. He dwelt there in tents as a temporary resident. This land was to be his promised inheritance. But he lived there as a stranger because he was looking expectantly and confidently ahead to the city God was building. Abraham's vision, trust, and endurance made him a great leader. He was truly the father of the faith.

Are you willing to follow the Lord as Abraham did? Do you consider yourself a foreigner in this world?

Prayer: Father God, thank You for being concerned for Your daughters in the faith. Like Abraham, I am thankful for this eternal home You have promised. Keep my vision steadfastly on you.

Day 6

"God, the blessed and only Ruler, the King of kings and Lord of lords, who alone is immortal and who lives in unapproachable light, whom no one has seen or can see. To him be honor and might forever" (1 Tim. 6:15-16).

We fight the good fight of the faith because of this heavenly vision— God is the only sovereign Ruler. No one has seen Him yet, but we wait for the appearing of our Lord Jesus Christ. Then we will know Him perfectly.

For now we maintain a spiritual perspective that compels us to obey and honor the King of kings. Our eyes are not on this world, and its values, but set on seeing Jesus and only Him. As leaders we must always adhere to and present the vision of His lordship. It corrects our near-sightedness while living in the world and compels us to righteousness.

Our kingdom perspective enables us to live our lives worthy of the Father who calls us to share the inheritance of His Son. Seeing ourselves as beloved daughters of the King, and living in that light keeps us motivated and accountable.

Have you thanked God lately for rescuing you from darkness? Does your perspective of the kingdom life motivate you to please Him?

Prayer: Sovereign and holy Lord, we long to see You clearly, but for now it is enough that we know You are King. We are Your servants. We want to do Your will.

DAY 7

"'We must go through many hardships to enter the kingdom of God'" (Acts 14:22).

One way Christian leaders can strengthen people is to help them realize that hardships are a normal part of the Christian life. Expecting the instant gratification of our wishes and prayers leads to discontent and loss of vision. When we accept the wait for God's answer, we can experience peace even in the most difficult circumstances. Thus, we share in the fellowship of Christ's suffering. He promises to sustain us and work for our good in all situations. If those we lead have a kingdom perspective of suffering, they are able to trust the Lord even more.

As believers we must establish our heaven-mindedness. We do not accept the world's attitudes. We aim to do the Father's will, pleasing Him by obeying the King. He knows everything we need and because He loves us He gives us His kingdom.

How do you accept hardships in light of your faith? Do you pray for and encourage others to trust God when they are faced with stress and difficulties?

Prayer: Heavenly Father, I know that even when life is hard, You are with me, side by side. Thank you.

FOR FURTHER REFLECTION

1. Old and New Testament Bible characters displayed courageous faith and so held expansive vision. They saw beyond human limitations and earthly circumstances to God's vision and purpose for their lives (Heb. 11). List six Bible characters below which particularly impress you and write beside each name the Bible's assessment of their faith and vision.

a. Read the following verses and describe the vision each Bible character possessed:

> Noah (Gen. 6:9—7:23)
> Abraham (Gen. 12:1-5; 18:1-19; 22:1-19)
> Joseph (Gen. 37:1-29; 50:15-21)
> Rahab (Josh. 2; 6:22-25)
> Mary Magdalene (Luke 8:1-3; John 19:25;
> Matt. 28:1-10; John 20:1-18).

b. What obstacles did each character overcome to fulfill God's vision for his/her life?

2. Look up the following verses and explain why faith is imperative to the realization of God-ordained vision.

> Matthew 8:5-13; 15:21-28; Romans 4:16-25;
> Colossians 1:3-6

Pray that God might give you clarity of vision in each area of leadership in your life and increase your faith daily, trusting Him to accomplish His purposes.

3. List the areas in which God has called you to leadership today. In one sentence of twenty words or less describe your "vision" for each area.

List three goals you desire to implement to see this vision fulfilled. Example: As a mother, my vision is to lead my children daily into a deeper relationship with Christ.

a. Pray and read the Bible daily with my children.

b. Listen to their report of daily activities and concerns and offer biblical directives for problem solving.

c. Spend fifteen to thirty minutes alone with each child each day.

NOTES

[1]Merrill J. Oster, *Vision-Driven Leadership* (San Bernardino: Here's Life Publishers, 1991), 13.

[2]Ibid.

[3]Donna Callea, "I Do Firmly Resolve," *The Sunday News-Journal*, Daytona Beach, Fla., January 2, 1983.

[4]Leroy Eims, *Be a Motivational Leader* (Victor Books, 1988), 41.

[5]Charles Swindoll, *Quest for Character* (Portland, Ore: Multnomah Press, 1987), 98.

[6]Leighton Ford, *Transforming Leadership* (Downers Grove: InterVarsity Press, 1991), 99.

[7]Ibid., 99, 100.

[8]Leroy Eims, *Be the Leader You Were Meant to Be* (Victor Books, 1988), 58, 59.

[9]John Naisbitt and Patricia Aburdene, *Megatrends 2000* (Avon Books, 1990), 321.

[10]Ibid.

[11]John White, *Excellence in Leadership* (Downers Grove: InterVarsity Press, 1986), 56, 57.

Establishing priorities and seeking God's perspective for leadership both demand personal evaluation. As we continue our study of leadership qualities, let's turn our attention to integrity. Examining our life-style for actions consistent with an attitude of truth is imperative for effective leadership. Personal, unwavering integrity will be reflected in everything and everyone our leadership influences.

J. Robert Clinton defines integrity this way:

> At the heart of any assessment of biblical qualifications for leadership lies the concept of integrity—that uncompromising adherence to a code of moral, artistic, or other values that reveals itself in sincerity, honesty and candor, and avoids deception or artificiality (according to Webster, Merriam Co.). The God-given capacity to lead has two parts: giftedness and character. Integrity is the heart of character. [1]

In this chapter, we'll define *integrity*, explore ways to evaluate integrity, and address difficult issues concerning integrity. A life of integrity stands in stark contrast to the teaching of the world today. Leadership with integrity testifies to our unflinching faith in Jesus Christ.

—*L. R. M.*

CHAPTER 4

WALKING IN INTEGRITY

Georgia Settle

Georgia Settle is a speaker and the author of the Bible studies *Women in the Bible* and *Seasons of Change, Seasons of Grace.* A Bob Jones University graduate and former secondary school teacher, she is a part-time employee for the Presbyterian Church in America's Christian Education and Publication Committee (CEP). She and her husband Paul have two children and one grandchild.

"I urge you to live a life worthy of the calling you have received" (Eph. 4:1).

By what standard is a life judged to be "worthy"? That cannot be answered without an understanding of Paul's reference to the calling which we, like the Ephesians, have received.

In the context of Paul's letter, we see that we are made alive in Christ, called to be His disciples, followers of His teachings. Our calling is to become more and more like Christ; therefore, the only standard by which our walk can be examined is the life and teaching of Christ.

He said, "I am the way, the truth, and the life" (John 14:6, KJV). His followers seek to walk in His way, to lift up His truth, and to reflect His life in all their circumstances and relationships. This is the essence of Christian integrity: all of life given to and focused upon Christ.

The Hebrew word for *integrity* is also translated "wholeness." Funk and Wagnall lists "undivided or unbroken" as one definition. We might use the phrase "all of one piece" or "a person who is not two-faced."

Among the synonyms of integrity are found character, honor, virtue, and fidelity. Isn't it interesting how modern culture has dropped or twisted all of these terms? The concept of "word of honor" is actually laughed at today; to speak of a person's character is to suggest that she is eccentric; and who even dares speak of virtue today?

Natural men, the ones who have not accepted Jesus Christ as their Savior, do not understand spiritual things; and we realize that integrity, when seen as a quality of the inner life of a person, must be viewed as a supernatural fruit of the Holy Spirit.

Definitions add to our understanding of integrity. For example, *virtue* is defined as "goodness, or the disposition to conform to the law of right." It is possible to conform outwardly to codes of morality for public impression or for personal gain, but the person of integrity is disposed in his or her heart to do what is right.

One definition of *fidelity* provides a graphic illustration for Christian leaders. The term is used to speak of "the accuracy and freedom from distortion with which a sound-reproduction system will receive and transmit the input signals."

So we ask, with what fidelity do we receive and transmit the Word of God? Would anyone say of us what the Sadducees said of Christ in Mark 12:14? "Teacher, we know you are a man of integrity. You aren't swayed by men, because you pay no attention to who they are; but you teach the way of God in accordance with the truth."

A person of integrity does not bend the truth or standards of conduct to fit different situations or people. This was graphically illustrated for me when I was teaching in a public junior high school.

One evening my class was rehearsing a play in the school cafetorium. When I was busy with the cast on stage, a few students took some ice cream bars from the school kitchen, ate some, and gave some to other students. When I discovered the incident and confronted them, they confessed. I told them to report to the principal's office the next morning and tell her what they had done. After consideration the principal instructed me to give them an "F" in conduct for that grading period.

The four students were all members of the school's honor society, attractive young men, and leaders among the student body. The other members of the honor society voted to drop them from membership.

One of the young men remarked sadly, "I don't get in trouble often, but when I do, it is really bad." In contrast, another of the involved boys, whose parents hired a lawyer to protest the principal's decision to the school board, stood in class the last day of school and said, "What I have learned in this class is that it does not pay to tell the truth."

The chairman of the board (who was a church officer) visited the principal (who was a member of the same church) and told her that, because of the political influence of the family involved, he might not be able to save her job unless she changed her ruling.

The principal said, "Unless you can show me that those boys did right, I cannot alter my decision."

Education was a career of great importance to that lady, yet she laid it on the line because she would not bend her standards under pressure. She did not lose her job, but she was willing to sacrifice it if necessary. Her example was an inspiration to me, to the school board, and to that student body.

Truth does not change with circumstances—neither do leaders who have integrity.

THE SOURCE OF INTEGRITY

In John 15, we read the beautiful word picture that describes the life flowing from the vine (Christ) through the branches (believers) to produce spiritual fruit in the heart and life. Christ said to His disciples: "He who abides in Me, and I in him, he bears much fruit. If you abide in Me, and My words abide in you, ask whatever you wish and it shall be done for you" (vv. 5, 7, NASB).

If then we speak of virtue or integrity as rare qualities, where can they be found? What is the source of goodness? Have you ever known someone whom you consider to be a genuinely good person? There are people that this phrase brings to my mind. Does it make you think of someone? Then let me ask, "What would you think, how would you feel, if that person were revealed as being dishonest or to be practicing some dreadful sin?"

As Bible believers we know that God's Word says that "there is none good, no not one." Someone said, "But that's speaking of our need of salvation." Yes, but when we accept Christ, do we become good?

No! Christ's goodness is credited to our account, but we will never be good in and of ourselves. If our lives appear good to others in any area, we must all remember that it is only because of the life of Christ within us! In Matthew 19:17, Christ reminded His questioner that the adjective "good" is applicable only to God.

In his book, *Transforming Grace,* Jerry Bridges writes:

> Every aspect of our ministry, whether it be an obscure ministry to one person or a public ministry to thousands, is by the grace of God. No human worthiness or adequacy is required or accepted . . . But it is all of God's bestowing. Every thought, word, or deed emanating from us that is in any way pleasing to God and glorifying to Him has its ultimate origin in God, because apart from Him, there is nothing good in us . . . Our best works are accepted to God only because they are made acceptable by the merit of Jesus Christ.[2]

So what should our response be when someone we deem good falls into sin? We grieve over the harm done to the testimony of Christ, but we should not be overwhelmed. Since all are capable of such sin, these incidents should humble us and make us aware of our own vulnerability. It is only God's grace that enables anyone to withstand temptation. He is the source of integrity.

Perhaps one of the greatest dangers accompanying positions of church leadership is that of beginning to believe what others say about you and taking personal credit for it. If at any time or to any degree a Christian begins to believe that the source of goodness is in her rather than in Christ, then she is in danger of relying upon her own strength, of neglecting the Word and prayer, and of becoming disillusioned and a source of disillusionment to others. God's grace made available to us in Christ is the only source of any good fruit borne in our lives.

INTEGRITY OF HEART

"Keep thy heart with all diligence; for out of it are the issues of life" (Prov. 4:23, KJV).

The Lord expects of His children hearts that are totally devoted to Him. When asked about the greatest commandment in the law, Christ replied, "You shall love the Lord your God with all your heart" (Matt. 22:37, NASB).

Integrity is defined as "undivided and unbroken" and that is what God requires of us—integrity of heart. Without obedience to this first and greatest commandment, no other obedience is acceptable to God.

Is there a contradiction when I profess to love God with all my heart and then tell my husband that I love him with all my heart? Of course not; it is only as I love God with all my heart that I am enabled to love anyone else as I should. First John makes it very clear that love for God requires that we love other believers. Conflict arises only when our love for others takes precedence over our love for God.

Yet how easy it is for our hearts to become divided by the cares of life and the things of the world. So much of our time must be given to things that take our focus from God. Keeping our hearts turned toward God should be our primary occupation. Everything in the world, our culture, and in ourselves fights against single-hearted devotion to God.

Jeremiah wrote, "The heart is more deceitful than all else and is desperately sick; Who can understand it?" (Jer. 17:9, NASB). J. C. Ryle said, "The seeds of every wickedness lie hidden in our hearts. They only need the convenient season to spring forth into a mischievous vitality."[3]

This fact should move us to pray daily and diligently for Christian leaders throughout the world, to examine ourselves continuously in the light of God's Word, and to remind ourselves constantly that the only way any of us are kept from sin is "by the power of God through faith" (1 Pet. 1:5, KJV).

The concept of integrity of heart before God is sometimes spoken of as commitment or having a "heart on fire for God." John Calvin pictured this in the logo he chose for his life—a burning heart in an open hand with the words, "I give my heart to Thee, O Lord, promptly and sincerely." To keep our heart with all diligence is to fan the flame of love to God and to obey Him from the heart.

INTEGRITY OF CONDUCT

The Lord said to Solomon in 1 Kings 9:4, "As for you, if you walk before me in integrity of heart and uprightness." These two things are mentioned together a number of times in Scripture. A righteous life is the product of an undivided heart.

Faith that does not result in a changed life is a very questionable faith. "As the body without the spirit is dead, so faith without deeds is dead" (Jas 2:26). It is impossible for a person to have a heart on fire for God without the light and warmth being seen and felt by others.

As we feed the fire in our heart by studying God's Word, by spending time with Him in prayer, by focusing our thoughts upon Christ, and by worshiping Him together with other believers, we will find ourselves growing more like Him in our attitudes and actions. The standard God has established for our conduct is His own holiness. He said, "I am the LORD your God. Consecrate yourselves therefore, and be holy; for I am holy" (Lev. 11:44, NASB). Christ said that those who follow Him are to be like salt and light.

In Micah 6:8 we read, "He has showed you, O man, what is good. And what does the Lord require of you? To act justly and to love mercy and to walk humbly with your God." In other words, the condition of our heart will be reflected in our actions toward others.

In the book *Loving God,* Charles Colson says, "So Christianity is not just a high-sounding ritual we perform on Sunday morning. Christianity is abiding by biblical standards of personal holiness and in turn seeking to bring holiness into the society in which we live."[4]

So we see that integrity means that our heart and our actions are all one piece. They are not divided in the sense that we live our life to fit what we profess to be in our heart.

This was not true of the Pharisees whom Christ described as "whitewashed sepulchers"—painted white on the outside but inside full of dead men's bones. We may try to hang the fruit of the spirit on our lives like ornaments on a tree, but unless the fruit grows out of the life of the Spirit within our hearts, it will wilt and fall off. Only as the branch abides in the vine can it produce rich and lasting fruit to God's glory (John 15).

INTEGRITY OF LIFE

"Therefore do not go on passing judgment before the time, but wait until the Lord comes who will both bring to light the things hidden in the darkness and disclose the motives of men's hearts" (1 Cor. 4:5, NASB).

In teaching, my husband has sometimes used an illustration about judging others. On a clean chalkboard, he will put a single small dot and ask, "What do you see?" Invariably someone in the group answers, "A spot." He asks, "Is that all?" Others will call it a dot or a mark, but seldom does anyone say, "A chalkboard with a spot on it."

When we look at another person's life, we often tend to judge him by one or two actions that stand out, ignoring the overall pattern of that life. We sometimes tend to judge ourselves in the same way and expect a perfection that we will never know on this earth.

King David is a good example of this. The sinful episode in his life involving Bathsheba and Uriah makes it hard for us to be objective about him. That incident is like a spot that draws our eyes from the rest of his life, the overall pattern of wholehearted devotion to God. Put into words, his psalms relate every believer's experience in their walk with God. God alone sees the heart and passes a final judgment.

As we observe the lives of other believers and look for evidences of integrity, we must be careful that we do not condemn anyone on the basis of isolated incidents. Even when we take into consideration the pattern of another's life, we should not pass or voice final judgment about their salvation.

Believers are told by Paul to "speak the truth in love." Do we not show a lack of integrity when we gossip about the lack of integrity in the life of another believer? When in conversation we refer to other believers it should never be with malice or harsh judgment. Every breach of integrity we see in the life of a Christian should drive us to our knees before God to seek His forgiveness and His grace to live out His righteousness before others.

As Christ dwells in our hearts by faith, we are united in Spirit with all those in whom He dwells. Let us pray for one another that the integrity of the church of Jesus Christ may be evident to the world.

THOUGHTS FOR DAILY MEDITATION

For I am God, and there is no other. By myself I have sworn, my mouth has uttered in all integrity a word that will not be revoked: Before me every knee will bow; by me every tongue will swear.

They will say of me, "In the Lord alone are righteousness and strength" (Isa. 45:22-24).

Isaiah and all the prophets spoke of God's uncompromising righteousness and justice. He is the only source of integrity. He is integrity.

The Father personally sent His Son from His presence to show us Himself. Jesus is integrity personified. He is the truth. He is steadfast and real. He relies on the Source and becomes our Source.

Honesty, wholeness, perfection, and truth are virtues that define integrity. If we are called to lead God's people, we must know and seek the source of this righteousness. We have access through faith to the Source, Jesus Christ. Without this reliance on God, our ministry will soon fail. Its success depends on the integrity that only God can provide through the Holy Spirit of Christ Himself.

Day 1

"'Teacher,' they said, 'we know you are a man of integrity and that you teach the way of God in accordance with the truth. You aren't swayed by men, because you pay no attention to who they are'" (Matt. 22:16).

The Pharisees plotted to entangle Jesus in His talk. They were commending Him for His integrity while trying to trap Him. Jesus was uncompromising. His rebuke was just—"you pretenders" (v.18, AMP). They had knowledge without understanding.

Does your leadership reflect God's integrity? Do you look to Him as your only source? Have you allowed the knowledge of God's truth and integrity to change your life? Are you swayed by men to compromise?

Prayer: Heavenly Father, show me my faults that keep me from a loving relationship with You. Help me to reflect Your Truth, rejecting the influences of the world that might weaken my integrity.

Day 2

"I know, my God, that you test the heart and are pleased with integrity. All these things have I given willingly and with honest intent. And now I have seen with joy how willingly your people who are here have given to you. O Lord, God of our fathers, . . . keep this desire in the hearts of your people forever, and keep their hearts loyal to you" (1 Chron. 29: 17-18).

David knew the importance of wholehearted devotion to the Lord. It gave him great joy to see the people he led give freely to God. He prayed their hearts would always be directed toward Him. God loves to show mercy and lovingkindness to His children who are completely devoted to Him. He established His covenant with us, and faithfully keeps it. Our part is to walk before Him with integrity.

The Lord tests our heart for integrity. Nothing pleases Him more than when we are upright. Of course, our dependence on Him and Christ's righteousness assures our success. His commands guide us as we go.

Are you wholeheartedly devoted to God? Can He delight in your uprightness?

Prayer: Lord Jesus, thank You for integrity based on Your righteousness alone. Keep us steadfast in our dependence on You.

DAY 3

"The integrity of the upright guides them, but the unfaithful are destroyed by their duplicity" (Prov. 11:3).

Once our source of integrity is established in the Lord and our hearts are set on Him, our integrity will affect our conduct. Honesty, faithfulness, morality, and justness will guide our living. The rightness of our hearts will be displayed in our action. Integrity produces abundant living.

In a like manner, deceitfulness has its effect. The lives of the unrighteous are ruined by their double-dealing. We must continue to walk with integrity and guard against our human bent for deceit. Devotion to Christ is our protection.

What guides you? Are you faithful in truth?

Prayer: Protect us, O Lord, from deceitfulness. Fuel our devotion for You. Guide us with Your integrity that we will be faithful and honest in all our conduct.

DAY 4

"In everything set them an example by doing what is good. In your teaching show integrity, seriousness and soundness of speech that cannot be condemned" (Titus 2:7-8).

We are to model good deeds having the greatest regard for truth and purity, to put our opponents to shame. If we abide by this high standard, they will have nothing with which to discredit us. The Holy Spirit enables us to maintain this standard. The integrity in our conduct reveals the reality of Christ's righteousness to the world.

Our faithfulness in handling worldly things proves our trustworthiness to handle spiritual riches. Little things of life are the testing ground for our integrity.

Is there any truth to your opponent's accusations? Do you model Christ's purity?

Prayer: Dear Lord, I want to be a model of purity and integrity. Help me to overcome any deceitfulness in my dealings with others.

Day 5

"'As surely as God lives, who has denied me justice, the Almighty, who has made me taste bitterness of soul, as long as I have life within me, the breath of God in my nostrils, my lips will not speak wickedness, and my tongue will utter no deceit . . . til I die, I will not deny my integrity'" (Job 27:1-5).

Job was tested to a degree few of us will ever experience. He understood God's sovereignty and trusted Him in all circumstances. One thing he guarded even unto death was his integrity. Job was upright and honest, and would speak no deceit. In all his suffering he remained true to his conscience. What an example! The trials of our lives are the proving grounds for integrity. As we are pressed on all sides with all kinds of adversity, the truth of who we are comes to light.

What trial is God allowing in your life to test you? Will you guard your integrity?

Prayer: Father, help us to be like Job. We know You understand our weaknesses, yet whatever adversity we encounter empowers us to remain true to You.

Day 6

"Judge me, O Lord, according to my righteousness, according to my integrity, O Most High. O righteous God, who searches minds and hearts, bring to an end the violence of the wicked" (Ps. 7:8-9).

David had been trained well to lead God's people. From tending ewes and their young, he was chosen to shepherd beloved Israel. He guided them skillfully with discernment. The Lord knows how to prepare His leaders. He looks at their hearts and develops their hands.

David knew God's judgment was just and pervasive. There was no hiding from God. God knows each heart and mind. The wise will honestly submit to God's searching and look to Him for righteousness. The wicked will face His judgment, too. We will all see justice done.

Do you allow the Spirit to search your heart and mind? What does He find?

Prayer: Heavenly Father, search my heart and mind and reveal to me the thoughts and deeds that are wicked in Your sight. Help me to change.

DAY 7

"In my integrity you uphold me and set me in your presence forever" (Ps. 41:12).

There is security in walking in truth. We can have peace and assurance. Walking on a crooked path means sure defeat.

God keeps us in our integrity. And the final result of remaining true is being set in His presence forever. There we find fullness and joy. *Selah.*

How does the Lord support you? Consider the result of living with integrity. Consider the alternative.

Prayer: Lord, I've considered the benefits of following Your guidance and found them wonderful. Uphold me in Your presence, I pray.

FOR FURTHER REFLECTION

1. In a culture that equates personal integrity with narrow thinking and repressive ideas, we must reevaluate our lives according to God's standard, His Word. God created us and knows what produces healthy, fulfilled living. Read the following verses and write phrases which give insight on integrity.

1 Kings 9:4-5; 1 Chronicles 29:17; Job 27:3-6;
Psalm 7:8; 25:21; 41:12; Matthew 22:16; Titus 2:7

a. Read Psalm 78:72. From your knowledge of David's life, give examples of his leadership described in this verse.

b. Read Proverbs 10:9; 11:3; and 13:6. What impact does integrity have on leadership as described here?

2. J. Robert Clinton, in his book, *Making a Leader*, lists what he calls "integrity checks." An "integrity check is a test that God uses to evaluate intentions in order to shape character."[5] Clinton explains that values determine convictions. Convictions are tested through times of temptation. Assaults by others against our vision of ministry tests our faith.

Making choices in response to God's guidance tests our calling. Persecution tests steadfastness, our ability to be loyal tests our allegiance, and making restitution tests our honesty. What situations in your life are being used as "integrity checks" for you today? Describe one.

3. First Corinthians 10:13 provides great comfort and assurance as we face the world's influence (Rom. 12:1-2) and Satan's onslaught (1 Pet. 5:8).

a. Confess any sin in your life which hinders you as you seek to live a life of integrity.

b. Pray for God's power and protection to maintain a leadership style exemplifying integrity in every area.

NOTES

[1] J. Robert Clinton, *Making of a Leader* (Colorado Springs: NavPress, 1988), 58.

[2] Jerry Bridges, *Transforming Grace* (Colorado Springs: NavPress, 1991), 168-69.

[3] J. C. Ryle, *More Gathered Gold* as compiled by John Blanchard (Evangelican Press, 1986), 139.

[4] Charles Colson, *Loving God* (Grand Rapids: Zondervan, 1983), 146.

[5] Clinton, 58.

The fourth specific quality for a woman in leadership is the ability to motivate others to reach their fullest potential. Recognizing their strengths, providing opportunities for developing these, and trusting the individual's ability to perform is all a part of motivating with insight. We must help others see their potential, seek the empowering Holy Spirit, and give them clear steps for realizing their goals.

J. Oswald Sanders, in his outstanding book *Spiritual Leadership*, writes:

> The spiritual leader, however, influences others not by the power of his own personality alone but by that personality irradiated, interpenetrated, and empowered by the Holy Spirit's undisputed control in his life; the Spirit's power can flow unhindered through him to others.[1]

Causing others to recognize this truth equips them to accomplish God's will. "Motivating with Insight" offers biblical directive for stimulating others to experience their fullest potential in Christ. It describes qualities of leadership which lack this insight and examples for better leadership.

—*L. R. M.*

CHAPTER 5

MOTIVATING WITH INSIGHT

Susan Hunt

Susan Hunt is an author, speaker, and consultant for the Christian Education and Publications Committee of the Presbyterian Church in America. She has written training manuals for women, *Leadership for Women in the Church,* and a children's alphabet book. Her latest book, *Spiritual Mothering,* is a call for Christian nurturing. She and her husband Gene have three children and two grandchildren.

"For we are God's workmanship, created in Christ Jesus to do good works, which God prepared in advance for us to do" (Eph. 2:10).

The 1991 Atlanta Braves baseball team became known as the "Miracle Braves" because they went from "worst to first." In 1990 the Braves were last in their league. In 1991 they won the National League championship. Jack Llewelyn, a sports psychologist, played a part in this success.

Pitcher John Smoltz was struggling. Llewelyn, employed to work with him, videotaped Smoltz pitching a perfect fast ball, a perfect curve ball, slider, etc. Over and over, day after day, Smoltz watched the video. Then whenever he got into trouble on the mound, he "replayed" the video in his mind. Visualizing a perfect pitch helped him deliver.

Smoltz had the technique and the ability, but he needed to feel confident that he could throw a strike in a difficult situation. The problem was not *competence* but *confidence.* Llewelyn recognized this and provided the confidence builder. John Smoltz went on to lead the Braves to the World Series.

Before we can motivate other women, we need to produce some mental videos. A woman of faith who desires to motivate other Christian women to obedient living needs to recognize that each one has competence in Christ. The motivator's role is to help others develop the confidence to serve Him. She needs to visualize them as God's workers doing the good works He prepared in advance for them to do. Then she needs to give them a copy of the video!

MOTIVATING WITH INSIGHT

Motivating with insight is a critical part of wise leadership. To lead means to show the way. To motivate means to stimulate to action. The two go together. Every Christian woman has opportunities to lead. In the home, church, community, or marketplace, our various relationships offer potent possibilities to show the way and to stimulate to action. But the question is, how do we do it?

First, we must recognize that without the internal motivation of the Holy Spirit we can, at best, only elicit short-term behavioral change. Only God's Holy Spirit can replace the "heart of stone" with a "heart of flesh" (Ezek. 36:26). Until the Holy Spirit performs this heart transplant, external motivation is powerless. Trying to motivate a heart of stone is as futile as it sounds. So what can we do? We can pray. Prayer gives us access to the most powerful change agent in the universe.

When God extends His grace and changes a heart of stone to a heart of flesh, the recipient of that grace will be ready to follow and able to learn a new way of life. Christian women are often blocked from maximizing their potential because they do not understand the power of the Holy Spirit within them. This is where the "video" comes in. Just as John Smoltz had the technique and the ability, Christian women have the Holy Spirit. But they lack the confidence to "throw the strike."

Many Christian women struggle with the I'm-not-good-enough-smart-enough-talented-enough syndrome. A leader of women understands that every daughter of the King has been uniquely designed and equipped for a purpose. She helps women embrace this perspective about themselves, then challenges them to squeeze every ounce of potential out of each ability and situation.

A young single woman in my Sunday School class has experienced dramatic spiritual growth during the last few months. Prior to this "growth spurt" I suggested various ministry opportunities to her. She was polite but never interested. Then God's grace exploded in her and lit a fire in her heart for serving others. One of the first ministries she volunteered for outside the church was a ministry to teens.

She tackled it with enthusiasm, but I was saddened when she shared her experience with me. The people in positions of leadership almost squandered this beautiful resource. Rather than spurring her on to love and good deeds, they abandoned her to discouragement and guilt. I am confident this was unintentional, but my sadness runs deep because I wonder how many others, in how many other ministries, are having this same experience because those who are leaders do not know how to motivate with insight.

How was my friend discouraged? She was given a vague assignment with neither instruction nor support. Not equipped to do what she was expected to do, she didn't produce. The disappointment of those in charge was clear. As a result, she felt discouraged and guilty. A ministry that promised great excitement and challenge became a source of failure and frustration.

PLANNING TO MOTIVATE

But now consider a positive example of a young woman whose potential was maximized because of godly leadership. Esther, a young Jewish girl who became queen of Persia and was used of God to deliver her people from annihilation, is a stunning example of obedience. Her classic statement, "I will go to the king . . . And if I perish, I perish" (4:16), has inspired women throughout the ages. I think, however, that we are often so captivated with Esther that we miss the rest of the story.

Esther's cousin Mordecai was a master motivator. We can learn from Mordecai as he shows us how to motivate women to seize the opportunities before them. Let's look at his action plan to motivate Esther.

First, Mordecai's entry into the picture didn't occur suddenly when the Jewish people were threatened. Instead "Mordecai had taken her as his own daughter" (Esth. 2:7) when Esther was orphaned. He accepted this little girl, loved her as his own daughter, and made a significant investment in her life.

When Esther was taken into the king's harem, Mordecai did not abandon her. "Every day he walked back and forth near the courtyard of the harem to find out how Esther was and what was happening to her" (v. 11).

While Esther lived in his home, Mordecai faithfully instructed her. Esther trusted this instruction and put it into practice when she was taken into the king's harem. "She continued to follow Mordecai's instructions as she had done when he was bringing her up" (v. 20).

When Esther became queen of Persia and her husband issued an edict that all Jews were to be killed, Mordecai appealed to her to be the advocate for her people before the king. Mordecai loved Esther. Asking her to take such a risk must have been a difficult decision. But she was in the most strategic position to be used in this crisis, so Mordecai recognized that as God's providential plan.

Motivating with insight factors in current situations and opportunities as well as abilities. Mordecai's challenge was not given in a vacuum. It was presented in the context of a caring relationship. We continue to see his wisdom in the way he presented the challenge.

When the appeal was made, Esther understandably hesitated. The risks were great. Mordecai persisted. His challenge reveals his penetrating insight.

"Do not think that because you are in the king's house you alone of all the Jews will escape. For if you remain silent at this time, relief and deliverance for the Jews will arise from another place, but you and your father's family will perish. And who knows but that you have come to royal position for such a time as this?" (4:13-14).

It is often assumed that the power of his challenge is in the words, "And who knows but that you have come to royal position for such a time as this?" But I believe that Mordecai's opening statement is what motivated Esther to obedience: "If you remain silent at this time, relief and deliverance for the Jews will arise from another place."

When the threat of annihilation came, Mordecai could say with assurance that deliverance would come with or without Esther. The sovereign God who had entered into a covenant relationship with Abraham would not allow His people to be annihilated. Mordecai spoke words that reminded Esther to reach back to what he had taught her about the character and promises of Jehovah and to act upon those promises.

Mordecai influenced Esther to make a decision to obey God. This decision was immediately followed by a request for support. Mordecai honored Esther's request and mobilized the people of God to fast and pray for her.

In the book, *Leadership for Women in the Church*, which I coauthored with Peggy Hutcheson, we wrote, "Consider the genius of Mordecai in motivating his young cousin to make herself available for kingdom work."[2]

First, notice what he did not do.

He did not devastate her by rebuking her, "If you were really committed you would not hesitate to assume this responsibility."

Neither did he use guilt, "I've done so much for you—you really owe me."

Nor did he build up a false confidence by focusing on her own abilities, accomplishments, or circumstances, "Esther you are so successful and loved—you can do it!"

Mordecai wisely realized that the overwhelming importance and anger of this situation was beyond Esther's internal resources. He instilled confidence in Esther by focusing her on the person and promises of God and by surrounding her with the prayers of God's people. This formula positioned Esther to confidently serve God and his people.

Mordecai was indeed a master motivator. When Esther came into his home he had no clue that she would play a vital role in Jewish history, but perhaps he did recognize the situation as an opportunity from God. Rather than viewing Esther as an intrusion and a burden, perhaps he had a mental picture of her being used to serve God. As he taught her of her heritage and the promises God had made to His people, perhaps he helped her to visualize herself responding to Jehovah's faithfulness in obedience regardless of the circumstance. Then, when the crisis came, she replayed the video and delivered the strike.

Mordecai's godly leadership was a significant factor in Esther's life and in the life of the Jewish community. His strategy is worth repeating:

> ➤ Establish a caring, nurturing relationship.
> ➤ Give biblical instruction. Influence the thinking before expecting the action.

➤ When there is a need for service, consider the abilities and current circumstances of women. Then present the opportunity.

➤ Give a clear description of the need and the expectations (a written job description).

➤ After presenting the opportunity, refocus on the person and promises of God and give assurance of your prayer support.

How does Mordecai's methodology translate into our experience? What does it look like in the lives of women today? It happens when women take the initiative.

Janet notices a young woman entering church with two small children and introduces herself. As they walk to the nursery, Janet learns that Martha is recently divorced. She sits with Martha in church, invites her and her children to lunch, and follows up during the week with a telephone call. Janet invites Martha to Bible study, often includes her and her children in family outings, and gives emotional and spiritual support. Martha flourishes spiritually and after a few months is instrumental in beginning a support group for single parents.

Peggy, the coordinator of the women's ministry, meets with the chairmen of the various committees and they leave the meeting energized. Peggy's excitement about the opportunities to serve the women in their church is infectious. Her sincere appreciation for what each of them contributes to the ministry, and her verbal affirmation of their efforts, is stimulating.

Judy, a woman in her fifties, meets with Diane, a young woman expecting her first child. Diane did not come from a Christian home, but wants desperately to honor the Lord as a Christian. During these weekly meetings, the women talk about being a wife and mother. Judy shares homemaking skills; they pray, study, laugh, and cry together. And Diane is gradually shaped into an obedient woman of faith.

Cathy, a stay-at-home mom, tells Anne that she would like to be involved in a ministry but has no spiritual gifts that would be useful. Anne learns that Cathy was a graphic artist and immediately connects her with the people on the church staff who can utilize Cathy's skills. Soon the church's newsletter and publicity have a professional appearance, and Cathy's artistic skills have been translated into a ministry.

These are pictures of motivating with insight.

Christian womanhood is at risk in our culture today. Women are hearing many voices with dazzling messages of self-actualization, self-fulfillment, self-promotion, and all the other "self" approaches to life. We are in desperate need of women of faith who are willing to courageously stand against sin and stand for righteousness. But it is not enough for us to make this decision for ourselves and to carry the banner alone. We must motivate others to follow.

Christian women need to have a vision of other women confidently and boldly serving the Lord God. We need to challenge them to lives of virtue and servanthood in order to glorify our glorious God. We cannot issue the challenge in a vacuum. We must be willing to make the investment, to give faithful instruction, to nurture, then to sound a clarion call to biblical womanhood.

Toward the end of the fourth century B.C. the Jewish nation was in jeopardy. Esther, motivated by Mordecai, stepped forward and served her God by being the advocate for His people before the king. The deliverance is celebrated to this day in the Jewish community in the festival of Purim.

Now, nearing the end of the twentieth century, Christian womanhood is in jeopardy. Are there women who will step forward and bring their lives under the authority of God's Word regardless of the risks? I believe there are. And I believe these women will stand in such stark contrast to the image of womanhood that is being flaunted today that they will shine as beacons in the darkness.

The warmth and beauty of that light will be so appealing that others will follow. And together we will celebrate our deliverance from death and destruction. Together we will celebrate a resurgence of virtuous living among the daughters of the King.

THOUGHTS FOR DAILY MEDITATION

"We have not *received* the spirit of the world but the Spirit who is from God, that we may understand what God has freely given us" (1 Cor. 2:12, emphasis added).

When we received the Holy Spirit at conversion, we obtained direct access to God's power. That power works in our lives to sanctify us. It works through our lives to enable us to minister. We tap this power by maintaining a right relationship with God. Our obedience to His commands and our submission to His will allow us to be filled continually with His Spirit.

The real source of effective leadership is reliance on the Holy Spirit. God has given Him to lead us into the knowledge of the truth so we too can lead others. To motivate them with insight we must rely on the Spirit's work both in us and in them. He is the one carrying out God's plan for our lives.

The Spirit directing and controlling our lives proves we belong to Christ. His power to work in us allows us to reject the power of the world and live for God.

DAY 1

"Having believed, you were marked in him with a seal, the promised Holy Spirit, who is a deposit guaranteeing our inheritance until the redemption of those who are God's possession—the praise of His glory"(Eph. 1:13-14).

This new life in Christ, directed by the Spirit, is an ongoing process. We grow in it by choosing to continue in step with Him, having our conduct controlled by Him. Reliance and perseverance are the keys.

The Holy Spirit is God's pledge to us, assuring us of our heritage in Christ until our redemption is complete. That will be a glorious day. But for now we have this foretaste of what's to come—the Spirit of God in us. God's promise was fulfilled to send a Helper and mark His servants.

Are you in step with the Spirit? Have you considered your inheritance in Christ? Does your conduct give evidence of the Spirit's control to those you lead?

Prayer: Gracious Father, stand beside me and help me to look forward to Your blessed inheritance.

DAY 2

"But the Counselor, the Holy Spirit, whom the Father will send in my name, will *teach* you all things and will remind you of everything I have said to you" (John 14:26, emphasis added).

The Father sent the Holy Spirit in Christ's place to represent Him. The Spirit is called Comforter, Counselor, Helper, Intercessor, Advocate, Strengthener, and Standby. In addition, He reminds us of Jesus' words when we need to remember! Considering that kind of help, we'd be foolish not to rely on Him completely as we lead others.

What needs do you have today that the Holy Spirit can satisfy? Have you remembered Jesus' assurance that the Spirit is with you always?

Prayer: Father, cause me to rely on the Holy Spirit's power within as I face daily demands. Help me to lead others to rely on Him.

DAY 3

"Paul, . . . to Timothy my true son in the faith" (1 Tim. 1:2).

Caring relationships are fundamental to Christian leadership. Christ's purpose in dying on the cross was to establish our relationship with the Father. During His ministry on earth He closely related to His disciples and especially to those who became the apostles, the leaders of His church.

Paul considered Timothy his son in the faith. Paul's paternal love was the basis of his concern, his instruction, and his exhortation to Timothy. The letters Paul wrote to him evidence this personal and affectionate care.

Our first responsibility in leading is loving. Our caring relationships validate and enhance our authority as leaders. Without love we are clanging cymbals.

What is the foundation of your leadership? Have you established loving relationships with those you lead?

Prayer: Gracious Lord, help me to be aware of the needs and concerns of those I supervise. Guide me to be a loving, aware leader.

DAY 4

"I give you this charge: Preach the Word; be prepared in season and out of season; correct, rebuke and encourage—with great patience and careful instruction" (2 Tim. 4:1-2).

Paul had established a loving relationship with Timothy. He supported him with prayer. He helped him discover his gifts. He nurtured him with sound teaching and by his own example. Now he charges

Timothy with his specific and sacred duty to zealously plead the Word at all times in every condition.

Sound teaching is vital to discipleship. Timothy not only heard the truth from Paul but saw it lived out in his life. As leaders we are required to teach the truth, to live the truth, and guard the truth by the help of the Holy Spirit. Then those we lead can pattern their lives on a solid foundation.

What sacred duty have you been charged to accomplish? Is your teaching sound? Have you been willing to issue a charge to others?

Prayer: Gracious Lord and Father, help me to live and exemplify the truth so that others will be wise in following my leadership.

Day 5

"It is God who works in you to will and to act according to his good purpose"(Phil. 2:13).

Assured of the Holy Spirit's presence in the lives of those we lead and having nurtured our relationship with them, we must now establish their reliance on God. *The Amplified Bible* says, "It is God Who is all the while effectually at work in you—energizing and creating in you the power and desire—both to will and to work for His good pleasure and satisfaction and delight." He is the power Source that enables His work to be accomplished in our individual lives and in our daily work (ministry). Reliance on Him is essential.

As leaders we have a unique opportunity to point people to dependence on God. Developing their confidence in Him is perhaps the most rewarding aspect of leadership. He proves Himself able and faithful every time. Our reliance on Him also frees us from the futility and burden of self-effort. As we trust in Him, He will do it.

Do the people you lead rely on you or God?

Prayer: Thank You, Lord Jesus, that we can rely on You to accomplish Your work in us. Free us from any sense of independence. We trust You to have Your will and way in our lives.

Day 6

"Now it is God who makes both of us and you stand firm in Christ. He anointed us" (2 Cor. 1:21).

God establishes us in Christ, confirms us, consecrates us, and anoints us with His gifts of the Spirit. He makes us steadfast. If we believe that, we can relax, rest in Him, and forget self-effort.

God has an individual plan for every believer's life. Each of us is His work, recreated in Christ to become part of His prearranged plan. Because He is a loving God, we are assured that our part is good.

Which path are you following for your life? Are you helping those you lead to find God's plan for their lives?

Prayer: Gracious Father, thank You for Your guidance as I look for the special gifts You have given each person I lead.

DAY 7

"But the people that do know their God shall be strong, and do exploits" (Dan. 11:32, KJV).

Motivating with insight requires a unique perspective. People need vision to persevere. The effective leader provides that vision by making others aware of their commission in Christ.

The Holy Spirit motivates us from within; we are nurtured by the church and rely on God and His promises to live according to His principles. As we grow in our knowledge of God, we prove ourselves strong and able to work for Him. Our motivation is not self-fulfillment but a desire to advance His kingdom. As in Daniel's day, the people who belong to God stand in obvious contrast to those living by the world's standards. When we realize our sacred duty, we can be like Daniel and make a difference.

Have you motivated others with the Great Commission? Are your deeds advancing God's kingdom?

Prayer: Father, we want to be strong in Your might. Enable us by Your power to work for Your kingdom and glory.

FOR FURTHER REFLECTION

1. Each individual is gifted by God. Read the following verses and list areas of giftedness:

Romans 12:6-8; 1 Corinthians 12:4-30; 1 Peter 4:10-11.

a. List other biblical gifts, talents, skills, or qualities others possess which you as a leader could motivate them to use for God's glory. (Include biblical references when possible.)

b. Describe ways you can motivate others to use their gifts for God's purposes.

2. The power of the Holy Spirit alone equips us to accomplish anything of eternal significance. What do you learn of the Holy Spirit's power from the following verses?

Acts 1:8; Romans 8:11; 1 Corinthians 2:4

3. List ways to help others learn to draw on the Holy Spirit's power to implement their gifts and fulfill Christ's plans for their life (Eph. 2:10).

NOTES

[1]J. Oswald Sanders, *Spiritual Leadership* (Chicago: Moody Press, 1989), 36.

[2]Susan Hunt and Peggy Hutcheson, *Leadership for Women in the Church* (Grand Rapids: Zondervan, 1991), 103-5.

A motivational leader sees the complete picture and motivates others to do their part in accomplishing the primary goal. Encouragement is a key aspect in this motivation.

God is the God of encouragement. Because of the love and value He places in His people, He offers constant encouragement to each of us. Through the promises in His Word, His arrangement of life's circumstances, and the individuals He places in our life, He gives us the courage to continue with joy.

Taking personal interest in the individual, and encouraging her simply out of respect and love regardless of the task, is a gift each leader can offer.

Paul writes, "Therefore encourage one another and build each other up, just as in fact you are doing" (1 Thess. 5:11). As a leader, encouraging for action offers clear, practical ways you can develop the ability to encourage others effectively. Whether you have the gift of encouragement—"If a man's gift is . . . encouraging, let him encourage" (Rom. 12:8)—or if it is a skill you desire to cultivate, apply the principles found in this chapter and watch God use you to encourage and inspire others to flourish.

—L. R. M.

CHAPTER 6

ENCOURAGING FOR ACTION

Lucinda Secrest McDowell

Lucinda Secrest McDowell is a freelance writer and speaker. She has contributed to three books and published articles in more than fifty magazines. Both editor and assistant editor for Christian newspapers, she has served as a Bible teacher and conference speaker at churches, colleges, and camps in California, Washington, North Carolina, Connecticut, Massachusetts, and Virginia. She and her husband Michael have four children.

I hurried into the ladies' room on my way to the seminar. My husband, Mike, and I were in Atlanta for a conference featuring several excellent speakers, including Gordon and Gail MacDonald. In the three years since we had seen them, a lot had happened.

They were no longer leading the Christian organization in which Mike had served for twelve years. We, too, had moved on to a new career, new coast, and new baby. Since the MacDonalds had just taken a pastorate in New York City, I was looking forward to their seminar on "Reaching Secular People" and to catching up on their lives.

I literally ran into Gail at the sink. After a brief greeting, her first question was, "How is Justin adjusting to your recent move? I've prayed for him."

Amid the hundreds of people she knows, she remembered that our eldest son is handicapped and finds change difficult. Her concern encouraged me. But it did not surprise me. For many years, Gail has been the very model of a woman committed to the ministering power of encouragement.

Eight years prior, I read her words in *High Call, High Privilege* which admonished Christian leaders in the discipline of learning people's names: "Haven't you told people you really love them when you remember even their children's names?"[1]

Now here I was, on the receiving end of that love from an older woman I respect and admire. I realized how essential the power of encouragement is for any woman who truly wants to have an impact on her world.

Our biblical mandate is clear. "Let us encourage one another—and all the more as you see the Day approaching" (Heb. 10:25). Every Christian can and should be an encourager. Counselor Larry Crabb says, "Encouragement is not the responsibility of a gifted few; it is the privilege of every believer."[2]

Encouragement is also a key to effective leadership. Leaders who are able to identify areas of strength in others' lives and then offer encouragement spur others on to growth and fulfillment. If we really believe that, the lives of those around us will surely be transformed.

Occasionally someone will say that I am an encourager. Of course, I still have a lot to learn in this area, but it is true that I am able to encourage because I have been encouraged. So many times, under the weight of discouragement and defeat, someone's encouragement has given me strength to move ahead.

It comes in many forms—an unexpected note in the mail, God's Word in my daily devotion, Christian music, a spoken word of affirmation, or even a surprise casserole brought during the "pit hour." Because I know how much such things mean to me, I seek to become a minister of encouragement.

When I lived in Virginia I had several opportunities to view the filming of the "700 Club" and Sheila Walsh's "Heart to Heart" television shows. It was easy to notice that the Christian recording star has a real vision for encouragement as a ministry.

"I want to shine a light at the end of the tunnel and tell people who are in the dark, 'Please hold on. If you just knew what God has in store for you, you'd keep on walking,'" she says.[3] No doubt the catalyst for Sheila's desire to help others see the light is her own time "in the tunnel" a few years ago. Others helped her along and now it's her turn.

Defined by Webster's dictionary, *encourage* means "to inspire with courage, spirit or hope." In the Bible, Barnabas was known as the "son of encouragement." Out of the fullness of his own walk he poured himself out to help others.

Much of what I have learned about encouragement came from a friend I met in graduate school thirteen years ago. Jeanne Doering, author of *Your Power of Encouragement,* told me that when in college she became concerned with the negativity so pervasive during the late 1960s. To combat this, she and several Christian friends formed "The Barnabas Committee." They prayed for staff, faculty, and students and sent anonymous notes and small gifts.

She writes that it was completely unexpected when the message went out to the whole campus: *"Encourage one another!* We noticed others starting to do similar things. People responded with lifted spirits. The campus turned positive. And the amazing thing was this: as we concentrated on encouraging other people, we too were encouraged."[4]

Although Jeanne is a continent away today, she still sends me periodic notes of encouragement and challenges me to keep my balance in writing, speaking, and family life.

How can we become encouragers? I'd like to suggest four areas of focus. By no means an exhaustive list of ways to become a minister of encouragement, the following principles will lead to changed lives and open doors that lead to serving our Lord.

> ➤ We must encourage *from the heart.* Unless we are staying close to the Lord and being nourished by His Word, we will have nothing to give to others.
> ➤ We need to cultivate the ministry of *a word aptly spoken.* Well-timed words of affirmation and genuine praise can spur others on to confidence and success.
> ➤ We need to utilize *the written word* as a "gift that keeps on giving." Developing the discipline of sending short greetings or Scripture often gives just the booster shot that is needed.
> ➤ We need to recognize the power of *prayer and exhortation.* We must become serious about specific intercessory prayer. At the same time, we may often use exhortation to challenge another toward growth in new areas.

FROM THE HEART

I recently read about Joyce Simmons who started monthly "encouragement parties" in her Minnesota home. Women gather to produce notecards with rhyming verse, brainstorm about practical helps, and intercede for others through prayer. They have a vision for reaching their world through a ministry of encouragement.

Joyce writes, "If I hadn't been willing to examine each area of my life, I could never have begun the ministry of encouraging myself. And without the strength of this inner encouragement I never could have reached out to encourage others. I would have failed at the first sign of fatigue, given up at the slightest rejection, or doubted my faith during the personal struggles that are part of everyday life. After all, love cannot flow from an empty cup!"[5]

"For out of the overflow of the heart, the mouth speaks" (Matt. 12:34). If we are not fueling our inner fires daily with God's Word, prayer, and worship, it is all too easy for the fire to go out. What suffers is our confidence, attitude, and the ability to give encouragement to others. Therefore, it is a necessity to identify what encourages our spirits and then do it. Bible teacher Linda McGinn reminds me, "God knows the needs of every human heart. He provides His promises to meet those needs as we see, obey and trust Him with all our heart."[6]

For me, a period of quiet and reflection away from all responsibilities brings new perspective. Whether it's an hour or a day, I return refreshed with a desire to give. I also feel encouraged when I exercise my gifts and see God at work. And sometimes just having a date with one of my teenage sons, or taking my daughters shopping or to the playground gives me a surge of hope and gratitude. These help me remember the really important things in life.

Where do you seek help when life seems senseless? It helps to plan each day to do something special to lift your own spirits. Likewise, by being sensitive to others, you can learn the best way to affirm their value and encourage them. Biblical counselor Larry Crabb points out that "the effect of encouragement is to stimulate the hope that solutions exist for every problem and that, seen from an eternal perspective, life does make sense."[7]

A WORD APTLY SPOKEN

Our move to New England in winter helped me appreciate the old Japanese proverb that says, "One kind word can warm up three winter months." King Solomon said it this way, "A word aptly spoken is like apples of gold in settings of silver" (Prov. 25:11). Our words have great power—they can wound or they can heal. Anyone serious about leadership must learn how to affirm and admonish others verbally.

Pratt Secrest, a Christian businessman and my father, has seen this work many times. He tells of a staff meeting that he held one week when all his employees had been petty and irritable with one another.

As the meeting began, he passed each one a piece of paper containing the name of a colleague. My father then announced, "Today we will go around the room and complete this sentence with the name you picked. 'I am so glad _____ is part of our team! One thing I really appreciate about him/her is _____.'"

After doing this, a time followed where differences were set aside and affirmation flowed freely. Daddy said that working conditions improved greatly. Six months later employees still commented about how much those words had changed their attitudes. We can do the same thing in our homes, on our committees, and in our churches. It is especially important to respond to a prompting of the Holy Spirit by saying it now. Tomorrow could be too late.

Yet there are times when we are hesitant to be honest. My friend Jeanne Doering has learned to be obedient to the Spirit's promptings to voice her affirmation of others. "For me it helps to preface a remark with 'Can I be serious and tell you something I appreciate about you?' or 'At the risk of embarrassing you, I'd like to tell you something very special.'"8

Is there someone in your life who needs a word of praise or affirmation? that behind-the-scenes secretary? your kids' new youth pastor? a seventh grade daughter who just got braces and glasses? or (lest we forget) your husband? Give them a verbal blessing today.

THE WRITTEN WORD

As I opened the airline magazine, an article caught my eye: "The Lost Art of Letter Writing." Skimming it, I pulled my tray down, took stationery from my purse, and began the task I planned earlier—writing notes to friends and family. The "high tech" nineties might prompt us to wonder why we bother to write a letter when a telephone is nearby. I disagree. Not only does the written word encourage over and over again, but, in a letter, we often speak more honestly and from the heart. So I write.

Ever since I first went away to college twenty-two years ago, my parents encouraged me by writing to me every week. Some shy away from this form of encouragement because they don't know what to say or they feel they must write a long letter. But often a few sincere lines on a postcard may be welcomed with joy.

I buy plain postal card stock by the pound, decorate it with a sticker or creative stamp, then affix postage. Every week or so I make a list of those near and far who may have a special need, and I put their address on the card. Often it is the name of someone on my prayer list, a minister whose sermon I appreciated, a soloist, or a missionary friend. It may be a surprise greeting urged spontaneously by the Holy Spirit.

Then I carry these addressed and stamped cards with me all week and write on them as short spaces of time open up in my schedule. When I don't know what to say, in the case of grief or tragedy, I use Scripture, hymns, and quotations.

One of my spiritual mothers, Elisabeth Elliot, has encouraged me this way endless times. Last year, in the midst of pain and disappointment, I received a postcard from her:

Well, Cindy, my dear, she wrote, *the Lord has again trusted you with a great trust. I am reminded of 2 Chronicles 20:12-22. He is the same Lord who heard the cry of His children, "We do not know what to do, but our eyes are upon you." No change should be cause for fright. He changes not. "Let nothing disturb you. Nothing frighten you. All things are passing. God never changes. Patience wins all things. Whoever has God wants nothing. God alone suffices" (Saint Teresa). Take only one day at a time. My prayers are with you all.*

Her words spoke to my heart that day and many days since, enabling me to press on and regain an eternal perspective. I also have shared Saint Teresa's words with several others since then.

PRAYER AND EXHORTATION

Several years ago I was invited to speak at a women's conference at Windy Gap, one of my favorite spots in the Blue Ridge Mountains. Hundreds of women were to come from nineteen states, and much preparation was involved. I soon learned that every week during the two months prior to the retreat, a small group of women would meet to pray over the names of every registrant and program participant.

I began attending these prayer times to go through the lists of as-yet-unknown women, believing that God would know how to touch them in the most needed ways.

Talk about a retreat bathed in prayer! During our weekend together, the Spirit moved in a mighty way, and women told many stories of God's divine intervention to get them there. All of us were encouraged to know we had been prayed for by name!

One woman professor says, "By prayer, we channel God's grace to those we love."[9] As women in leadership we should be channels of grace.

When we promise to pray for someone, we must do it. I believe in immediate and specific prayer and often respond to prayer requests by offering to pray right then and there—whether it is on the phone, the freeway, or at a party. Nothing encourages us to give our best effort more than knowing the power of someone's prayers is behind us.

Another form of encouragement is exhortation, or the "kick in the pants" kind. I am so grateful that I have friends who encourage me to act by challenging me to take risks and try new things. They also keep me sharp by prodding me to maintain a larger world view.

Miriam Adeney, who juggles the study of missions, marriage, and motherhood, is just such a friend. In her book on priorities for women, *A Time for Risking,* she challenges women today to become acquainted with the foremothers and Christian sisters who demonstrate all that is beautiful and strong to stimulate us to stretch ourselves also.

"That doesn't mean idolizing them," she writes. "Take Mary Slessor (a nineteenth-century missionary to West Africa who came to be known as Eka Kupkpro Owo—'the mother of all the peoples'). She had her faults. She was bossy and cranky with co-workers. She was not a team player. Her theology was rudimentary as were her teaching methods. So what else is new? Of course she had her weaknesses. Because of these very limits her witness hit close to home. In Mary, as in other foremothers, we see what a fairly common woman can do who dares to be strong. Who dares to be creative. Who dares to blaze."[10]

Has a sister shared a dream with you lately—one so big it would take a mighty act of God to accomplish? You can encourage her in two ways today. First, pray for her, and with her if possible. Second, with honesty and helpful recognition of her strengths, challenge her to take a giant step of faith and action.

THOUGHTS FOR DAILY MEDITATION

"I am the vine; you are the branches. If a man remains in me and I in him, he will bear much fruit; apart from me you can do nothing" (John 15:5).

Encouraging others requires a vital union with Christ, the Source of all encouragement. Women in leadership must nurture their relationship with Him in order to strengthen those they lead. Just as the branches that are rightly connected to the vine bear good fruit, we bear the fruit of encouragement when we are rightly connected to Jesus. But being *rightly* connected is the key. Daily devotion to Christ through prayer and Bible study builds us up and enables us to reach out to others. When we neglect our relationship with Him, we have little to give.

Encouragement means to inspire with spirit and confidence. By remaining close to Christ we are nurtured and inspired with confidence. His Word replenishes us. So we must learn to rely on His Spirit in order to be effective as a minister of encouragement.

Day 1

"As the deer pants for streams of water, so my soul pants for you, O God. My soul thirsts for God, for the living God" (Ps. 42:1-2).

We are designed to long after God and the streams of living water He provides to quench our inner thirst. Through Christ's death, we have ready access to these streams at any time. To receive the help we need, we are able to enter boldly into His presence at any time. To be strengthened with power, the Bible tells us we can draw on Christ's unlimited riches and resources. Imagine it. Our potential is limitless. His Holy Spirit indwells us and enables us to accomplish His will.

Who do you long for? Have you allowed the Holy Spirit to invade your life with His power?

Prayer: Gracious Father, quench my thirst with Your living water. I pray You will hear the needs of my heart and help me be an encourager.

DAY 2

"The tongue has the power of life and death" (Prov. 18:21).

Our words may have the power of life and death. As encouragers of women we should be aware of the effect of our spoken words. The Bible has much to say about our speech. It's important that we speak from the heart and are willing to reveal our true self. Again, our relationship with God and our dependence on Him are vital to successful, encouraging leadership.

Peter admonishes us to speak the words of God. A sobering challenge, but it is possible if we are Spirit-controlled and seeking to please Christ. We have a sacred responsibility to serve God with our words. The Scriptures tell us that by controlling our tongue we prove the value of our faith. We cannot curse man and bless God. Are the words you speak words of life? Does the Spirit control your tongue?

Prayer: Holy Spirit, we yield our tongues to You. Enable us to please the Father and bless man with our words.

DAY 3

"Preach the Word; be prepared in season and out of season; correct, rebuke and encourage—with great patience and careful instruction" (2 Tim. 4:2).

We have an urgent message to declare to others. We need to be prepared at every opportunity to speak the words of Christ with patience. With perseverance we are to warn, encourage, and convince others to do what is right.

A godly woman's words have value. Her advice is worthwhile, faithful, and truthful. A godly woman's counsel is given with kindness and life-giving to those who listen.

How does your counsel measure up? Are you prepared to herald His message at every opportunity?

Prayer: Dear Lord, thank You for Your message of good news. Prepare me to deliver it in Your name.

DAY 4

"Have not I written to thee excellent things in counsels and knowledge?" (Prov. 22:20, KJV).

The significance and power of the written Word are shown throughout the Old and New Testaments from the law of Moses to the names written in the Lamb's Book of Life. Excellent counsel and knowledge are written to be remembered by the present generation and passed on to future ones.

God's written words to us, and ours to others, are a powerful means of encouragement. They can change lives and bring comfort and inspiration. Do you read God's message of love regularly? Do you write it to others?

Prayer: Jesus, Author of all things, write Your Word on my heart and help me to extend Your words of life to encourage others.

DAY 5

"The Word became flesh and made His dwelling among us. We have seen His glory, the glory of the One and Only who came from the Father, full of grace and truth" (John 1:14).

Jesus is the Father's Word to us: His living Word, bringing the timeless message of His love for all people. The Bible tells us that some refused to receive His message. Even today that is true. Ears are dulled and hearts are hardened to the Word from God's heart. Though seated at the Father's right hand in heaven, Christ is among us. He is living in us. His words of grace and truth have not changed, but now as His disciples we are His script to the world.

Is your life an example of lovingkindness and truth? Does it reflect Jesus' words? What message do you give those who read your life?

Prayer: Dear Lord, grant that my words and deeds will be acceptable in Your sight, that my life will reflect the message You have given Your children.

DAY 6

"Therefore confess your sins to each other and pray for each other so that you may be healed. The prayer of a righteous man is powerful and effective" (Jas. 5:16).

James refers to prayers that heal and restore spiritual health. Accompanied by the confession of our offenses and pleas for forgiveness, prayers for others are part of the treatment God prescribes for our "sin sickness." Praying for others is a required ministry for every Christian, especially those who lead. The writer of Hebrews states that Jesus lives to intercede for us. He is our example to imitate.

Prayer is our link to the throne of grace. *The Amplified Bible* translates, "earnest (heartfelt, continued) prayer of a righteous man makes tremendous power available." Prayers of passion and perseverance activate power. Encouragers can do no greater work than pray for others. Does your prayer life include confession? Are your prayers for others heartfelt? Do you persevere in prayer?

Prayer: Merciful Father, we thank You for the work of Christ enabling us to enter Your presence. Hear our prayers for Your children.

DAY 7

"Encouraging, comforting and urging you to live lives worthy of God, who calls you into His kingdom and glory" (1 Thess. 2:12).

Paul instructed and exhorted the Thessalonians to live a life that would please God. We, too, can learn from his methods.

A man that ran the one-quarter mile race in high school said his coach's strategy was to run the first half as fast as he could, and the second just a little faster. Exhort others—urge them to give their utmost in running their race, to do their best over and over to please God.

Effective encouragement is essential for Christian disciples. Who wouldn't respond to comfort and urging that is done in love? Those who lead should be encouraged to live lives worthy of the great God they serve. Christian leaders are called to kingdom living for His glory. Are you living a worthy life? Do you exhort, comfort, and urge with His irresistible love?

Prayer: Dear Heavenly Father, guide and direct me so that I may become Your source of encouragement and comfort to many.

FOR FURTHER REFLECTION

1. From these verses identify the source of all encouragement.
2 Thessalonians 2:16,17; Romans 15:4-6;
a. Explain the goal of all encouragement as seen in:
Colossians 2:2; Hebrews 3:12-14; 10:24-25.

b. How is the ministry of encouragement applied in:
Acts 15:32; Colossians 4:7-8;
1 Thessalonians 3:2-3?

2. List four means of encouragement to offer those whom you lead.

3. Ask the LORD for wisdom and direction in identifying the needs of those you lead. Apply creative methods of encouragement to reach out to each individual.

Write the name of each woman you lead and list one way you can encourage her this week.

NOTES

[1]Gail MacDonald, *High Call, High Privilege* (Wheaton, Ill.: Tyndale, 1981), 162.

[2]Lawrence J. Crabb Jr., and Dan Allender, *Encouragement: the Key to Caring* (Grand Rapids, Mich.: Zondervan, 1984), 134.

[3]Jane J. Struck, "Out of the Tunnel," *Today's Christian Woman,* January/February 1992, 58.

[4]Jeanne Doering, The Encouragers (Christian Herald Books, 1982), 12.

[5]Joyce Simmons, *Shared Joy Is Double Joy* (Nashville, Tenn.: Thomas Nelson Publishers, 1985), 21.

[6]Linda R. McGinn, *Growing Closer to God* (Atlanta, Ga.: Great Commission Press, 1990), 114.

[7]Crabb and Allender, 80.

[8]Doering, 45.

[9]Miriam Adeney, *A Time for Risking* (Portland, Ore.: Multnomah Press, 1987), 105.

[10]Ibid., 159.

It's your attitude that determines the quality of your life, not your health,"[1] says Dr. Kate M. Smith, doctor of psychiatry, who has studied, from a woman's perspective, worldwide health problems and medical services.

Learning to see God's hand at work in every aspect of life is essential to successful leadership. Maintaining a positive attitude by focusing on God's active participation in all of life equips us to lead others to see God in our midst.

J. Oswald Sanders in his book, *Spiritual Leadership*, writes, "A pessimist never makes an inspiring leader. Hope and optimism are essential qualities for the servant of God as he battles with the powers of darkness for the souls of men. God's servant would be optimistic until His full objective is maintained."[2]

As we lead others to see life through God's perspective, we challenge them to see His sovereign work accomplishing His will for their good. Familiar verses like, "And we know that in all things God works for the good of those who love him, who have been called according to his purpose" (Rom. 8:28) and "he rewards those who earnestly seek him" (Heb. 11:6) hold new meaning as Christian women look for God's good work in each endeavor.

As you read Linda Tomblin's essay, "Implementing a Positive Outlook," consider ways God has enabled you to focus on His good provision in the midst of difficult situations. Consider each circumstance and each person under your leadership as you search for indications of God's will and work.

What can you find that is noble, right, pure, lovely, admirable, excellent, or praiseworthy in every moment of your daily life and work?

—*L. R. M.*

CHAPTER 7

Implementing a Positive Outlook

Linda Tomblin

Linda Tomblin, co-author of the book *Fingerprints of God,* is regional writer for *Guideposts* magazine and has ghostwritten more than one hundred articles for them. Many of her stories and articles have been published in Christian and secular magazines. A teacher for writers workshops and conferences, she is married and the mother of four children.

For years, I maneuvered in and out of life's problems trying my best to "think" good things into existence. And eventually I became firmly convinced that any man or woman could capture a healthy outlook on life if they'd just put their mind to it. I didn't realize who the true source of power was until I found myself lying on the examining table in the radiology department of our local hospital.

I wasn't really worried about the tests I'd undergone that Monday morning. In fact my biggest concern at that moment was whether or not I'd get out in time to pick up the clothes at the cleaners before they closed for lunch. Our family doctor had discovered what he thought was a small hernia near the spot where I'd had gall bladder surgery a few years earlier. So he'd sent me back to my surgeon, and the surgeon had ordered an abdominal scan to check it out.

But when the radiologist and his assistant walked over to the examining table after the tests, I could tell by the look in their eyes there was something else wrong. "You do have a small hernia," the doctor said, "but . . . . " his voice gentled as he looked down at me, "we've also found something else—a mass in your lower abdomen. It looks like a growth on your right ovary." I tried to keep my attention on what he was saying, but it was as if my mind stopped with the word *mass*.

He reached down and patted my arm. "We did a lower abdominal scan in addition to the ordered test. We do this occasionally for survey purposes," he said, "but, first things first, right now we need to get you over to ultrasound and see what they have to say."

As they escorted me to the ultrasound department, all I could think was, *this can't really be happening*. After all, I hadn't even been hurting. The most I'd expected was some simple surgery to take care of the hernia. But that was forgotten now, pushed aside. Then the surgeon came down to tell me he would set up an appointment with my gynecologist.

When I arrived home at 1:00, I found a message on our answering machine asking me to be at the women's clinic at 2:15. By 4:00 I was examined again, put through more tests, and scheduled for blood tests, an EKG, and surgery on Thursday morning.

Everything was happening too fast. My dependable positive attitude and thoughts disappeared. Instead I felt as if I'd been thrown on a runaway train of terror with no way to get off.

I spent the next two days calling my family, close friends, and relatives. Appointments were canceled and necessary arrangements made. I spent my nights lying in bed, staring at a dark ceiling and fighting off tears. In spite of reassuring words and arms ready to hug me close, the train picked up speed. No matter how hard I tried, this was one time I couldn't generate enough willpower to think confidently. In fact, I wasn't able to think or concentrate at all. The world seemed to be flying by without me, and all I could do was snatch quick glimpses as it passed.

Then the whispers inside me began. *Maybe you've been mistaken all along. Maybe there really isn't anything to maintaining a positive outlook after all. Maybe you just need to be strong and face up to what's coming.*

Even though my heart still argued, my mind began to agree. Early Wednesday morning I slipped out of bed and carried my Bible to the living room. The house was quiet as I skipped from passage to passage, book to book, trying to find something to reassure me, to help me during this time. While glancing through Philippians, I came to the words,

"Whatever is noble, whatever is right, whatever is pure, whatever is lovely, whatever is admirable—if anything is excellent or praiseworthy—think about such things" (4:8).

In those quiet moments alone in my living room, God told me to look at the good side, the positive side! I'd read that same Scripture numerous times before, but this time the words marched off the page and into my heart. God was showing me how to maintain a positive outlook by believing His Word. "Fix your thoughts on what is true and good and right."

In the quiet of the morning I asked God to direct my thoughts to the lovely, praiseworthy things He provided. I asked Him to help me appreciate His excellence so that there would be no room for worry and concern. Only then did my world slow from the blur of fear to a clear vision. I saw the things happening were true and right in spite of, or perhaps because of, my problem.

My family changed in those last few days. When I was speechless about the future, my husband told my children and friends what was happening. Our two older daughters made plans to help with the younger children and also to stay with me at the hospital when possible. Thirteen-year-old Katie and sixteen-year-old Andy assumed extra household chores when I had trouble functioning. When I finally began to look through God's eyes and focus on the good, I realized that the situation could be a time of growth for both my family and myself. It was an opportunity for our love to stretch and our faith to expand. "Think about things that are pure and lovely . . ."

Sitting there beside my window, I watched the stars disappear and listened to the birds waken. As the cool air drifted through the window on a silky breeze and as the sun began its morning climb over the distant mountains, I felt my first peace in days. As the sky filled with soft peach and orange, I forgot everything except the beauty and pureness of God's creation.

How long had it been since I rose early enough to watch the sunrise, I asked myself. *How long had it been since I sat and looked at the night sky, waiting patiently for the stars to sprinkle light through the dark?* When I followed God's instructions, my mind was filled with beauty, leaving no room for worry about tests that morning or surgery the next day. If

God loved me enough to give me the sunrise and the stars, surely I could trust Him with my life. "Dwell on the fine, good things in others."

My thoughts returned to the previous night. My brother-in-law had always been the "big brother" to our family, ready to lend a solid shoulder or steady hand. Now he was in bed with an incurable disease, unable to be a personal help. When told of our problem, his one thought was to make certain someone in his family would stay with our children in the waiting room during the surgery.

Turning from the window, I picked up a message pad lying beside our phone and for the first time noticed the list of calls from concerned friends, members of our church, and students from my writing classes. Many offered their help.

Now that I was seeing more clearly, signs were everywhere. Signs of loving, caring people—not because they felt obligated but because they sincerely wanted to help. I found a casserole a neighbor had dropped by, a freshly baked cake, and an encouraging note from the elderly residents at the rest home where my husband and I taught Sunday School each week. Even the doctors and nurses from the clinic and hospital were genuinely concerned and tried to make the arrangements as easy on us as possible.

Hope returned with the arrival of the casseroles, notes, and phone calls. Without knowing it, friends had become visible signs of God's invisible presence. "Think about all you can praise God for and be glad about" (Phil. 4:8, TLB).

With dawn came the knowledge that the ability to think good and confident thoughts comes only from God and that the praise belongs to Him. During the last few days, I learned that neither mind-set nor determination would enable me to "think" good things into being. Alone I was unable to imagine any possible good ahead for me. But in the peaceful silence of that morning, I realized for the first time that I didn't need tremendous amounts of willpower and that I wasn't alone. In fact, I had never been alone.

I returned to the Bible and read, "And the God of peace will be with you" (v. 9). I still had no idea where I was heading, but that no longer concerned me or mattered. Even though I was still frightened, inside I was filled with gladness that I didn't have to be in control. God was the conductor. He'd taken charge of my train of thought, and I was certain that in the future, no matter what happened, it would be a good ride.

THOUGHTS FOR DAILY MEDITATION

Let us fix our eyes on Jesus, the author and perfecter of our faith, who for the joy set before Him endured the cross, scorning its shame, and sat down at the right hand of the throne of God. Consider him who endured such opposition from sinful men, so that you will not grow weary and lose heart (Heb. 12:2-3).

Effective leadership requires a positive outlook of hope. Every situation in life presents the choice for a negative or positive response. Even for believers, a positive perspective may be hard to maintain when confronted by pervasive evil. Jesus is the answer.

We are to look away from all that distracts us from Him, the Leader of our faith. Christ, when faced with the cross, saw God's greater purpose and went forth in hope. Because of the joy before Him, He endured it, completely disregarding its shame.

We should carefully consider the Lord's example. His accomplishments on Calvary prompt and sustain our own attitude of hope. Instead of losing heart, we fix our eyes on Jesus and our faith grows stronger.

DAY 1

"I am the way and the truth and the life. No one comes to the Father except through me. If you really knew me, you would know my Father as well. From now on, you do know him and have seen him" (John 14:6).

Knowing that Jesus is the reality of truth, showing us who the Father really is, gives us a positive outlook for our lives. Jesus is the perfect expression of God's sincerity and character. Through Him truth is manifested in all its fullness. He is the essence of reality.

If we consider all that Christ represents, we can't help but have hope. He is heir and owner of everything. He created and arranged the universe and the ages of time. He is the image and glory of God. By His mighty Word He maintains and guides all of creation. Through His death and resurrection He accomplished our forgiveness and right standing before God. Now He sits at the right hand of the Father, interceding for us. As believers, how can our outlook be negative?

How do you see Jesus? Are you encouraged to know Christ is truth?

Prayer: Lord Jesus, You are the source of all my joy, confidence, and peace. Help me to reflect that in my dealings with others.

DAY 2

"But you, O Lord, are a compassionate and gracious God, slow to anger, abounding in love and faithfulness" (Ps. 86:15).

The Lord came down in a cloud passing in front of Moses to proclaim His attributes: sovereignty, compassion, mercy, grace, patience, lovingkindness, and faithfulness. These qualities became the prayer and pleas for all generations who believe. Relying on God's lovingkindness, we maintain an outlook of hope. We can trust Him with our whole life.

What should be our response to the Lord's mercy and His eternal faithfulness? Praise! All nations will praise Him. He extends His love to the whole world. But the beloved extol Him now and forever. Our praise can change our outlook from despair to joy. Praise Him, people!

Do you trust God enough? Will you offer a sacrifice of praise to God right now? Challenge those you lead to consider His faithfulness and praise Him, too.

Prayer: I offer my praise to You, O Lord. Thank You for being there when I need You and for Your loving concern.

DAY 3

"For since the creation of the world God's invisible qualities—his eternal power and divine nature—have been clearly seen, being understood from what has been made, so that men are without excuse" (Rom. 1:20).

Creation itself displays God's invisible attributes. All He has made speaks of His diversity and awesome power.

Examining the wonders of nature and all of creation reinforces God's majesty. Have you thanked God for the privilege of seeing His Person, character and wonderful attributes, demonstrated in creation? Can you see His majesty in its beauty?

Prayer: Almighty God, we are amazed at Your greatness as we look around us at Your creation. Help us to see You and rejoice with positive appreciation and joy.

DAY 4

"For you created my inmost being; you knit me together in my mother's womb. I praise you because I am fearfully and wonderfully made; your works are wonderful, I know that full well" (Ps. 139:13).

The final and most magnificent act of creation was the making of man. Here the psalmist tells us God is still intricately involved in our individual creation. He forms us in the womb. He plans our days before we're even born. In awe we worship this great God who knows us intimately and loves us in spite of our faults and failures.

When you realize that God had a plan for you before you were born, are you cooperating with His plan?

Prayer: Father, I thank You for having a plan for my life. Help me to be receptive as You reveal it through the days of my life. May I respond with the positive attitude of gratitude.

DAY 5

"God has combined the members of the body . . . so that there should be no division in the body, but that its parts should have equal concern for each other. If one part suffers, every part suffers with it; if one part is honored, every part rejoices with it. Now you are the body of Christ, and each one of you is a part of it" (1 Cor. 12:24-27).

Paul uses the body as an analogy to describe Christ's church. Just as human bodies need each part to function properly, we need each member of the body of Christ. Recognizing every member's value and importance, and esteeming their function promotes healthy spiritual growth. As we focus on what is good in each distinctive part, the whole body is built up. Each of us should have a mutual interest and care for the other members. We share in suffering and rejoicing alike.

The mark of Christ's body is love. Christ set the standard of that love by laying down His life for us. As leaders our love must dominate everything we do. We need to see the people we lead the way Christ sees them—completed in Him.

Are you willing to love others the way Christ loves you? Do you share in the honors given another believer?

Prayer: Jesus, help me to esteem each member of Your body, so I can positively build up and encourage each one to do Your will.

Day 6

"Give thanks to the Lord, for he is good. His love endures forever. Give thanks to the God of gods. His love endures forever. Give thanks to the Lord of lords: His love endures forever" (Ps. 136:1-3).

The praise of our God is a straight path to a positive outlook. As leaders we need with grateful hearts to focus continually on the Lord and who He is. We need hearts full of praises! He is Lord of lords and God of gods. He is more than worthy of our exaltation. His mercy and lovingkindness last forever. Consider His ways!

We can often be weighed down by circumstances and difficulties in our personal life or ministries. That's when we may lose our perspective of the goodness and praiseworthiness of God. Thanksgiving is a gate to His presence. Praise is a key to the sanctuary where we can again find joy. It restores our positive outlook and strengthens our competence to lead and minister to others.

Are you rightly joined to the power source? Are you giving thanks to our loving God?

Prayer: Lord, You are so worthy of our praise. With grateful hearts, we exalt Your holy name.

Day 7

"Sing joyfully to the Lord, you righteous; it is fitting for the upright to praise him. Praise the Lord with the harp; make music to him on the ten-stringed lyre. Sing to Him a new song; play skillfully, and shout for joy" (Ps. 33:1-3).

Praise is becoming an appropriate song for those who belong to God. The Hebrew word here means to "dance for joy," expressing heartfelt and living exultations. Music is a normal means to offer praise. We can sing joyful new songs to the Lord because we're righteous in Him. All His people great and small join in Christ to praise the Lord God Almighty.

We can rejoice because He reigns. We will give Him glory. As we look ahead to the marriage supper of the Lamb, let us practice praising Him with song and voice. Hallelujah, He is worthy.

Have you ever danced with joy in praise of Him? Do you join with others to offer Him praise?

Prayer: Lord Jesus, with all the people, I raise my voice praising Your name. I rejoice that You reign.

FOR FURTHER REFLECTION

1. Read Philippians 4:8 and list the qualities of life we are to focus our thoughts upon.

a. Describe a difficult situation you are confronting right now. Beside each of the qualities you found in Philippians 4:8, write one positive thing about this situation for which you can give thanks to God.

b. Read 1 Thessalonians 5:18. We may feel that we cannot give thanks *for* every life situation, but we can give thanks *in* all things. Pause and thank God now that you can trust Him to be at work in the midst of your situation. Pray and ask for an attitude that focuses on the qualities listed in Philippians 4:8 rather than negative thoughts that discourage and defeat.

2. Read the following passages, writing phrases that give insight into the mental attitude God desires for us.

Romans 12:2; Ephesians 4:22-24; 1 Peter 4:7

3. Prayerfully list three practical ways you can help those you lead capture a new attitude of hope and a positive outlook on life. Ask God to help you implement these ideas for the accomplishing of His purposes.

NOTES

[1]Betty Pettinger, "Attitude Is Said to Determine Quality of Life," *Richmond Times-Dispatch*, April 1978.

[2]J. Oswald Sanders, *Spiritual Leadership* (Chicago: Moody Press, 1967), 34.

Focusing our thoughts on the things that are true, noble, right, pure, lovely, and admirable as mentioned in Philippians results in a cheerful attitude, an attitude reflected in a bright countenance, genuine smile, and a sense of humor. All these bring joy to others and an atmosphere of warmth and pleasure.

Even in the most difficult circumstances, a sense of humor is essential to good leadership. In a recent women's magazine, the writer said, "Scientific evidence is mounting that a positive outlook and a sense of humor can bolster the immune system and enhance your health."

In a medical school study, ten students were asked to watch a humorous movie while ten others sat quietly in another room. The students who watched the movie showed a decreased level in the stress hormones which suppress the immune system. The level remained unchanged in those who had not seen the film.

The data supports the theory that a positive frame of mind, including feeling happy and laughing daily, produces beneficial physical effects, according to Dr. Lee S. Berk of Loma Linda University School of Medicine.[1]

Warren Wiersbe writes, "No matter what kind of disposition we were born with, the Holy Spirit can create within us a new heart and joyful spirit."[2]

Cheerfulness and joy permeate the Bible. Proverbs speaks of a "cheerful look" and "cheerful heart." In Timothy we read that God "richly provides us with everything for our enjoyment" (1 Tim. 6:17). Jesus prays for us in John 17, "but I say these things while I am still in the world, so that they may have the full measure of my joy within them" (v. 13).

How cheerful are your look and heart? As you read this chapter, ask God to give you new insight into ways to lead with joy.

—*L. R. M.*

CHAPTER 8

DISCOVERING A CHEERFUL ATTITUDE

Edna Edwards

Edna Edwards is general manager of Blue Ridge Broadcasting Corporation, a Christian radio station, and is a business woman, speaker, singer, and writer. She produces and hosts the devotional radio program "Manna in the Morning," which airs on WFGW Radio. Board member of National Religious Broadcasters since 1974, she is a graduate of Marion College, Indiana, and is married to Phil Edwards.

"Edna Jane, your attitude is awful! Just wait till your father gets home."

That's the first time I heard the word *attitude* from my parents. You may ask what the discussion was all about. I hated cleaning my room, especially when it was Mother's idea. That day she wanted it done. I dillydallied until she couldn't stand it any longer and took action. Immediately my sunny disposition disappeared.

When my father arrived home and was told about the situation, he called me into the living room. There he folded a sheet of paper down the middle. On one side he wrote GOOD at the top, and on the other he penciled BAD.

Together, we listed my good and bad traits and actions. Then he handed me the tally sheet. "OK, E.J., it's your decision," he said. "Remember you're Jesus' girl as you consider your good and bad actions."

The tally sheet became my guide far into the future. Analyzing it, I realized that my life would be much happier if I remembered to follow the "good" side. That person was optimistic, joyful, bright and sunny, and able to cheer others. With my father's reminder of Jesus and the list as a goal, my teenage outlook on life changed.

The Value of a Cheerful Attitude

During the exercise with my father I realized that a happy, cheerful attitude would be a benefit throughout my life. In Proverbs 15:30 I read, "A cheerful look brings joy to the heart, and good news gives health to the bones."

Likewise, Matthew Henry in his commentary states, "It is pleasant to have a good prospect, to see the light of the sun and by it see the wonderful works of God, with which this lower world is beautiful and enriched. . . . It is also very comfortable to hear (as some understand it) a good report concerning others." Commenting on Proverbs 17:22, he adds, "It is healthful to be cheerful. . . . It does good as a medicine to the body making it easy and fit for business."

The Attribute of Cheerfulness

Now, many years later, I am still finding new ways to upgrade my understanding of a cheerful heart. In God's Word, the contrasts are clearly described:

"A happy heart makes the face cheerful, but heartache crushes the spirit" (Prov. 15:13).

"All the days of the oppressed are wretched, but the cheerful heart has a continual feast" (v. 15).

"A cheerful heart is good medicine, but a crushed spirit dries up the bones" (17:22).

Speaking as a businesswoman, I have personally benefited in my work at Blue Ridge Broadcasting by remembering that a smile and happy, cheerful attitude help to create a peaceful environment.

For example, some time ago, I was greatly depressed because of concern for friends. My prayers seemed to rise no higher than the ceiling. My heart was heavy. Although trusting God was the answer, my faith seemed to be too weak to leave it to Him. Instead I worried constantly and the "down" feeling hung on. I was close to tears all the time.

One morning I decided to climb into bed, pull the covers over my head, and ignore the lovely day God had given. Then I remembered that yesterday I had turned the problem over to God. Why had I wrapped the problem back into a large bundle and now planned to carry it to bed with me?

God reminded me of Isaiah 41:10 where He assured Israel of His help. "I will strengthen thee; yea, I will help thee; yea, I will uphold thee with the right hand of my righteousness" (KJV). If He could do that for a rebellious group of Israelites, surely He could do it for me.

Looking into the mirror, I was shocked. My face looked sad and distraught. *Could it be that bad?* I thought. So, remembering my past blessings, I smiled at my reflection. Then I began to sing. I felt my spirits lift. After a cup of coffee, a bath, some face paint and fresh clothing, I headed for the office knowing that God had relieved me of my burden. He would carry it.

Experiencing the Joy of Surrender

It is true—not all of us are naturally endowed with a happy disposition. Yet, no one is attracted by a grouchy countenance. In my opinion, joy always follows when we accept His will. With God's guidance and our willingness to submit to it, we can depend on a cheerful attitude and a smile that is genuine.

In the midst of tremendous national problems, Abraham Lincoln wrote, "I have often wished that I was a more devout man than I am. Nevertheless, amid the greatest difficulties of my administration, when I could not see any other resort, I would place my whole reliance in God, knowing that all would go well, in that HE would decide for the right."

God's Control Produces Hope

My mother's favorite answer to most of my questions about life was a quote from a simple poem by an unknown author.

He knows, He loves, He cares—
Nothing this truth can dim.
He gives the very best to those
Who leave the choice to Him!

Some years ago, I heard a speaker relate an old Egyptian saying: "The archer strikes the target partly by pulling, partly by letting go. The boatman reaches the landing partly by pulling, partly by letting go."

Our attitude will change when we let go. It can be difficult. We strain, pull, and struggle, trying to hold on. Our hopes and plans for the future result in frantic anxiety when our problems would be solved if we let go and gave God the control.

Have you noticed that human efforts do not always achieve success? When we turn our anxieties over to God, His plans for us give the best direction for our lives. Our attitudes change when we accept God's superior plan. We are assured that miracles do happen when God takes charge.

This is most likely to happen when we pray for what God wants, not for our own desires. It happens when we ask God to use us for His purpose, not for our own successes. Paul says, "I have strength for all things in Christ Who empowers me—I am ready for anything and equal to anything through Him Who infuses inner strength into me" (Phil. 4:13, AMP).

What an excellent reason for a smile! The result—a cheerful attitude, of course.

THOUGHTS FOR DAILY MEDITATION

"All the days of the oppressed are wretched, but the cheerful heart has a continual feast" (Prov. 15:15).

A glad heart enjoys an ongoing feast despite circumstances. Cheerfulness is the attitude of optimism. It is a disposition of joy and hope based on heartfelt reliance on God. That reliance gives a positive outlook even in difficult situations.

Cheerfulness implies a willingness and promptness to respond with joy. The Bible often mentions the heart as the base of our emotions—the place where our attitude begins. If our heart is feasting on the goodness of God, joy and hope will spill out of our lives to affect others for good.

And the opposite is true as well. The days of the despondent are made miserable by anxious and foreboding thoughts. Their anxiety spills out and infuses others. As leaders we have a wonderful opportunity to cheer and inspire those we lead with joy and hope. Several times in Scripture Jesus Himself told His disciples to "take heart" and "be of good cheer" because He had overcome the world. We can feast on that assurance, knowing God is in control, enabling us to encourage others.

Day 1

"A cheerful look brings joy to the heart, and good news gives health to the bones" (Prov. 15:30).

A cheerful attitude is infectious. When our countenances and words reflect the joy we have in the Lord, it can't help but inspire others to experience that same joy.

Gladness of heart shows in our countenance, but a sorrowful outlook, without hope, breaks the spirit. Even in the most difficult situations, this gladness is not superficial when we depend on God for our guidance and help. It is hope and joy in Him that sustains us.

As we depend on God each day, He prescribes cheerful thoughts to bring healing to others. The contrast is obvious. If we approach our leadership with an unhappy, critical attitude, everyone will suffer.

Do your words bring healing? Are you relying on God for a cheerful heart even in adversity?

Prayer: Loving Father, help me to remain cheerful even when faced with adversity, knowing that You share the burden.

Day 2

"I have told you these things, so that in me you may have peace. In this world you will have trouble. But take heart! I have overcome the world" (John 16:33).

The Amplified Bible says the reason we can be confident and courageous in the midst of certain trials is because Jesus has deprived the world of power to harm us. He has conquered it. When our hearts are set on that fact, we can enjoy His peace. We now will have the courage needed to face whatever tribulations come our way.

This courage is one attribute of a cheerful heart—a heart that relies on Christ's finished work and sets its hope on Him. Several times in Scripture we see Jesus admonish His disciples to take heart, to be of good cheer. This word to them strengthened their faith. It gave them the determination they needed to persevere in even the most severe tests.

Are you facing frustrations and trials today? Do you draw courage from the example of Jesus overcoming the world?

Prayer: Jesus, thank You for Your overcoming power and finished work. Your peace and confidence are what I need for encouragement to endure.

DAY 3

"You will show me the path of life; in Your presence is fullness of joy, at Your right hand there are pleasures for evermore" (Ps. 16:11, AMP).

Five times in the New Testament, Jesus told His disciples to be of good cheer. When they were in a storm on the sea, fearing for their lives, they saw Him walking toward them on the water. His words were simple and profound, "Take courage! It is I" (Matt. 14:27).

Being rightly related to God is the foundation for our joy. Eternal pleasures are at the right hand where Jesus sits. His path for our lives is real life. True joy at its fullest is only found in His presence. As we delight ourselves in Him, accepting His will for us no matter what comes, we are rewarded by being filled with joy. Our joy can be a major attraction to those we lead, inspiring them to obedience and faithfulness.

Have you found the path for your life? Have you looked for and found Jesus in the storms of life? Do you take courage from His sovereignty?

Prayer: Gracious Father, thank You for being with me through the trials of my life. Help me to trust You completely.

DAY 4

"Yet I will rejoice in the Lord, I will be joyful in God my Savior" (Hab. 3:18).

Habakkuk's declaration to trust God no matter what calamity he might face attests to his keen faith. He not only trusted in God, but rejoiced in Him as well. In the preceding verses, he acknowledged his fear and anticipated the devastation to come. But his faith never failed. He knew he would be filled with joy because of God, his Savior, even though he also knew he faced adversity.

Jeremiah, too, feasted on God's words (Jer. 16:16). They sustained him and became his joy because he belonged to the sovereign Lord. We can all delight in the Word—His truth. If we belong to Him, it will become a joy to us.

When you face calamity or fear, do you, with faith, call on the Lord for support? Does your relationship with the Savior fill you with joy?

Prayer: Heavenly Father, I trust You. Please forgive my lack of faith and fill me with Your joy.

DAY 5

"I have told you this so that my joy may be in you and that your joy may be complete" (John 15:11).

The Lord Jesus has ransomed us to walk on the holy way—His highway to our everlasting joy. He has made the way for us to be overtaken by gladness. Here all our sorrow will disappear as we enter His presence with joy and praise.

The path to joy is obedience and abiding in love. Jesus instructs us so that we can be completed and overflowing with His joy and gladness. Being secure in our relationship with the Father by faith in Christ, we remain in Him by obedience to His commands.

Are you abiding in love? Does joy evidence your obedience?

Prayer: Heavenly Father, I trust You. Thank You for the joy of knowing and loving You.

DAY 6

"But the eyes of the Lord are on those who fear him, on those whose hope is in his unfailing love" (Ps. 33:18).

One way we revere the Lord is by setting our hope on Him. Everyday life has a way of distracting our hope. Often it's easier to put our expectations on people, or circumstances, or future achievements. When we do, we set ourselves up for certain disappointment.

However, those who hope in God's unfailing love will never be disappointed. Waiting on Him with trust assures us of success. He watches for such trust.

Putting our hope on *who* He is no matter what circumstances we encounter is our security. He never changes. He is always reliable, always loving, always merciful. As we continue to look through this dim glass, hope remains a key to our faith in Christ.

Do you practice hope? On what do you set your hope? During the hard times, do you put your hope in Him?

Prayer: God of all hope, we trust in You and Your unfailing love to see us through the good and bad times.

DAY 7

"We who have fled to take hold of the hope offered to us may be greatly encouraged. We have this hope as an anchor for the soul, firm and secure. It enters the inner sanctuary" (Heb. 6:18-19).

As a ship is held securely in place by its anchor, our hope secures us to the place Jesus entered on our behalf to the safety of God's presence. This anchor will not slip or break no matter what happens to us. If we flee to Him for our refuge, we will have the strength to hold fast to that hope. He is our hope.

Christ in you is the only hope for the glory to come. This great mystery is revealed to His people. We can rely on Him—Christ in us, by the indwelling of His Holy Spirit.

How do you hope to realize your promised glory? Are you securely connected to the safety of His presence?

Prayer: Dear God, thank You for being there when I seek refuge. Guide me through each day, enable my life to reveal the hope of the living Christ to all.

FOR FURTHER REFLECTION

1. Read Psalm 126:2. What did others see in the laughter of the Hebrew people?

a. How is joy, expressed in a genuine smile or laughter, a testimony to God's work in our lives?

b. Can you remember the last time you laughed with those you lead? Describe the situation.

2. What attitude or atmosphere typifies the meetings held with those you lead? Is your group typified by joy? Is your home, work, or committee inviting to others? Why or why not?

3. Read the following verses and write phrases that offer insight concerning cheerfulness and joy.

Proverbs 15:13,15,30; 17:22; Psalm 19:8;
Isaiah 55:12; Job 33:26; John 16:24; Philippians 4:4

4. List five ways you can relieve an atmosphere of tension and begin incorporating a cheerfulness among those you lead. Prayerfully ask God to help you implement the suggestions you proposed.

NOTES

[1]Lee S. Berk, "Laughter: Rx for Health," *First*, April 27, 1992, 33.

[2]Warren Wiersbe, "The Medicine of a Merry Heart," *Good News Broadcaster*, September 1985, 6.

A study by Priority Management, Pittsburgh, Inc., shows the life of the average person includes six months idling at red lights, eight months tearing open junk mail, one year searching for misplaced items, two years returning phone calls, four years doing housework, five years standing in line, and six years eating.

Time management is important to self-control and discipline. Does your schedule reflect set periods of time to accomplish the priorities God has revealed to you, or do you wander aimlessly from one activity to the next?

Henry David Thoreau once offered "first prize" to the man who could live one day deliberately. Ruth Ann Ridley writes, "Such a day would be a treasure. It would be a day in which other people's demands would not control our minutes, in which we could be flexible with quiet assurance, in which we would not be plagued by a maze of tumbling thoughts or by the 'devilish onrush' of time—a day in which we would order our ways rightly and experience God's help" (Ps. 50:23).[1]

Should this not be our desire? As a woman leading others, it is your responsibility to act with self-control and discipline. You offer an example for the accomplishment of God-ordained goals by ordering life activities and time commitment.

As you read Elisabeth Elliot's essay on discipline, ask God for wisdom to understand and strength to apply the principles of a self-controlled and disciplined life.

—L. R. M.

CHAPTER 9

Pursuing a
Disciplined Life[2]

Elisabeth Elliot

Elisabeth Elliot is the author of more than twenty-eight books. Her radio program, "Gateway to Joy," is heard on more than two hundred stations. Born in Brussels, Belgium, to missionaries, she graduated from Wheaton College. While in Ecuador as a missionary to the Auca Indians, her husband Jim was killed. Returning to the Aucas in 1958 with her daughter Valerie and Rachel Saint, Elisabeth continued the missionary work. She and her husband Lars have 8 grandchildren.

No story in the Bible captured me more powerfully when I was a child than the story of the prophet Eli and the boy Samuel. It was in the time when "The word of the Lord was seldom heard, and no vision was granted. Samuel had not yet come to know the Lord, and the word of the Lord had not been disclosed to him" (1 Sam. 3:1,7, NEB).

The child was sleeping alone in the temple, near the ark of God, when he heard what he thought was Eli's voice calling his name. Three times he ran obediently to his master; three times he was told that Eli had not called. At last the old prophet realized that it was the Lord and told the boy what to say next.

As with Samuel, God calls me. In a deeper sense than any other species of earthbound creature, I am called. And in a deeper sense I am free, for I can ignore the call. I can turn a deaf ear. I can say that no call came. I can deny that God called or even that God exists. What a gift of amazing grace—that He who made me allows me to deny His existence!

Discipline is the believer's answer to God's call. It is the recognition, not of the solution to his problems or the supply of his needs, but of *mastery*. God addresses us. We are responsible—that is, we must make a response.

103

Discipline is the wholehearted yes to the call of God. When I know myself called, summoned, addressed, taken possession of, known, and acted upon, I have heard the Master. I put myself gladly, fully, and forever at His disposal, and to whatever He says my answer is yes.

CHRISTIAN DISCIPLINE

Christian discipline means placing oneself under order. The disciple is one who has made a simple decision. Jesus invites us to follow Him, and the disciple accepts the invitation. I do not say it is an *easy* decision, and I have found that it needs to be renewed daily. The conditions are not such as attract multitudes. Jesus stated them: (1) one must leave self behind, (2) take up one's cross, and (3) come with Him.

The result of the decision is guaranteed. (1) Whoever cares for his own safety is lost, (2) but if a man will let himself be lost for My sake, he will find his true self. The disciple is not on his own, left to seek self-actualization, which is a new word for old-fashioned selfishness. He is not "doing his thing" to find his own life or liberty or happiness. He gives himself to a Master and in so doing leaves self behind.

DISCIPLINE OF WORK

There is no such thing as Christian work. That is, there is no work in the world which is, in and of itself, Christian. Christian work is any kind of work, from cleaning a sewer to preaching a sermon, that is done by a Christian and offered to God.

This means that nobody is excluded from serving God. It means that no work is "beneath" a Christian. It means there is no job in the world that needs to be boring or useless. A Christian finds fulfillment not in the particular work he does, but in the way in which he does it. Work done for Christ all the time must be "full-time Christian work."

"We shall not make any wild claims," Paul wrote to the Corinthians, "but simply judge ourselves by that line of duty which God has marked out for us, and that line includes our work on your behalf. We do not exceed our duty when we embrace your interests, for it was our preaching of the gospel which brought us into contact with you. Our pride is not in matters beyond our proper sphere, nor in the labours of other men" (2 Cor. 10:13-15, NEB).

What is our "proper sphere"? We cannot dismiss the fact of modern life; there are indeed many choices when it comes to discerning that sphere. Let us rest assured that God knows how to show His will to one who is willing to do it. The place to begin discovering the larger sphere is in the smaller one—in the willingness to say yes to every demand that the need of a neighbor makes us face.

What constitutes a "great work for God"? Where does it begin? Always in humility. Not in self-actualization but in self-surrender. Not in being served but in serving. I once heard a formula guaranteed to prevent boredom.

It is to have (1) something to do, (2) someone to love, and (3) something to look forward to. The Christian has all these in Christ: work, a Master, a hope. Yet how easily we forget this. One of the results of the fall is that we lose sight of the meaning of things and begin to see the world as dull and opaque, instead of charged with glory.

Even the work of writing ("Christian" books!) can become dull. It looks wonderfully exciting to many. I know because they come to me with eyes shining and speaking of how wonderful it must be.

But if they ask if I love to write, is it pure pleasure, do I ever find it hard, I must admit that for me the process is always hard. I must make myself tackle it, day after day. Yesterday, for example, was bad. I did not feel like working. That's what it came down to. I was restless, distracted, and disgusted with myself.

"Of making many books there is no end; and much study is a weariness of the flesh" (Eccl. 12:12, KJV) was the only verse that spoke loud and clear to me. I thought of all those Christian bookstores, filled with the avalanche of bright paperbacks that pour daily off the presses; of the full-color brochures and full-page advertisements for the newest blockbuster. Why add yet another book to the pile?

The job that surely is one of the world's pleasantest does not always hold much appeal to the one whose job it happens to be. It is difficult to keep in mind the spiritual character of our work (for there is spiritual character to all work that God gives us).

Work is a blessing. God has so arranged the world that work is necessary, and He gives us hands and strengths to do it. The enjoyment of leisure would be nothing if we had only leisure. It is the joy of work well done that enables us to enjoy rest, just as it is the experiences of hunger and thirst that make food and drink such pleasures.

So let us lift up our work as we lift up our hands, our hearts, our bodies—a sacrifice, acceptable because it is lifted up to Him who alone can purify.

DISCIPLINE OF THE BODY

The Christian's body houses not only the Holy Spirit Himself, but the Christian's heart, will, mind, and emotions—all that play a part in our knowing God and living for Him.

In my case, the "house" is tall; it is Anglo-Saxon, middle-aged, and female. I was not asked about my preferences in any of these factors, but I was given a choice about the use I make of them. In other words, the body was a gift to me. Whether I will thank God for it and offer it as a holy sacrifice is for me to decide.

The knowledge that the body will one day be "Sown as an animal body, . . . raised as a spiritual body" (1 Cor. 15:44, NEB) ought to give a disciple pause to think of the use he makes of it in this world. Even though flesh and blood can never possess the kingdom, think of its particles being "beckoned" to sit down with the Lord some day.

DISCIPLINE OF THE MIND

A simple and orderly life represents a clean and orderly mind. Muddled thinking inevitably results in muddled living. A house that is cluttered is usually lived in by people whose minds are also cluttered, who need to simplify their lives. This begins with simplifying and clarifying their thinking. Mind and life need to be freed from the "disorder of the unnecessary."

"Be mentally stripped for action, perfectly self-controlled," is what 1 Peter 1:13 (NEB) says we must do.

Jesus said that the greatest commandment is "Love the Lord your God with all your heart, with all your soul, with all your *mind*" (Matt. 22:37, NEB).

The transformation of the mind produces a transformed vision of reality. What the world calls "real" will lose its clarity. What it calls "unreal" will gain clarity and power.

Stories of men such as the apostle John or Saint Francis of Assisi cause the unrenewed person to say, "This man can't be real," forgetting that holiness is very real indeed. Holiness is, in fact, vastly more real, vastly more human than unholiness, being very much closer to what God created us to be.

A renewed mind has an utterly changed conception, not only of reality but of possibility. A turn away from the kingdom of this world to the kingdom of God provides a whole set of values based not on the human word, but on Christ's. Impossibilities become possibilities.

One of my husband's greatest gifts is friendliness. He meets people easily and quickly puts them at ease. I don't. He helps me by his example, and I am learning, but I also need his word. Recently he spoke to me about not having been as friendly as I should have been to a stranger. My immediate response to his remark was anger.

That particular stranger happened to be a young person who stopped me in a hotel and addressed me by a nickname used only by my family and old friends. My annoyance showed, Lars said, in spite of my having smiled, greeted her, and expressed an interest in what she was doing. Lars gave me a brief lecture. Nothing I didn't already know.

Why should he lecture me, I was thinking. *He has been impatient with people at times. And besides, that girl had no business . . .*

My reaction was "real." It was honest; that is, it certainly was what came to mind first. I said aloud none of the things I was thinking, but what I was thinking was in the old pattern, not the new, not the mind of Christ. "Reality" is often evil. I knew my thoughts toward this girl were wrong to begin with, and my thoughts as Lars was exhorting me were much worse. The Holy Spirit reminded me of the truth: let God remold your mind. Set your mind on heavenly things.

Think Christ was the new thought that came. Where did it come from? Not from me. Not from a secular mind-set. The Holy Spirit re-minded—*re*-minded—me.

"He who refuses correction is his own worst enemy, but he who listens to reproof learns sense" (Prov. 15:32, NEB).

"Lord, help me to face the truth of what Lars is saying to me, instead of blocking it out by self-defense," I prayed. I have found it necessary, sometimes deliberately, to refuse thoughts of what someone has done to me and to ask for help to dwell on what Christ has done for that person and wants to do for him and for me, for I am sure that my treatment of people depends on how I think about them.

The disciple who honestly seeks to let God remold her mind will direct her energies to a total surrender of obedient love. With her heart open to the Spirit of God, she will be in a position to learn wisdom.

DISCIPLINE OF TIME

I was brought up to believe that it is a sin to be late. To cause others to wait for you, my parents taught us, is to steal from them one of their most precious commodities. Time is a *creature*—a created thing—and a gift. We cannot make any more of it. We can only receive it and be faithful stewards in the use of it.

"I don't have time" is probably a lie more often than not, covering "I don't want to." We *have* time—twenty-four hours in a day, seven days in a week. Demands on our time differ, of course, and it is here that the disciple must refer to his Master. What do You want me to do, Lord? There will be time for *everything* God wants us to do.

There were endless demands on Jesus' time. People pressed on Him with their needs so that He and His disciples had not leisure even to eat, and He would go away into the hills to pray and be alone.

Still He was able to make that amazing claim, "I have finished the work you gave me to do" (see John 17:4, RSV). This was not the same as saying He had finished everything He could possibly think of to do or that He had done everything others had asked. He made no claim to have done what He wanted to do. The claim was that He had done what had been *given*.

This is an important clue for us. The work of God is appointed. *There is always enough time to do the will of God.* For that we can never say, "I don't have time." When we find ourselves frantic and frustrated, harried and harassed, and "hassled," it is a sign that we are running on our own schedule, not on God's.

Frustration is not the will of God. Of that we can be quite certain. There is time to do anything and everything that God wants us to do. Obedience fits smoothly into His given framework. One thing that most certainly will not fit into it is worry.

Direct your time and energy into worry, and you will be deficient in things like singing with grace in your heart, praying with thanksgiving, listening to a child's account of his school day, inviting a lonely person to supper, sitting down to talk unhurriedly with husband or wife, writing a note to someone who needs it.

Time management, a highly developed science today, begins for the Christian with time set aside for God. Other things cannot fall into a peaceful order if this is omitted. The best time for most people is early morning—not because most of us love jumping out of bed, but because it is the only time of day when we can be fairly sure of not being interrupted and because it is best to commune with God before you commune with people. Then your attitude toward others will arise out of your life in Him. Offering to God the first hour of the day is a token of consecration of all your time.

THOUGHTS FOR DAILY MEDITATION

"The Spirit of the Sovereign Lord is on me, because the Lord has anointed me to preach good news to the poor. He has sent me to bind up the brokenhearted, to proclaim freedom for the captives and release for the prisoners" (Isa. 61:1).

The good news prophesied in Isaiah is freedom from self-rule. God created that freedom and man's ability to yield to or resist it. Yielding means fulfillment and joy. When we say "yes" to God, He lovingly masters our lives. Discipline is that surrender to Him. If we resist, 'self' holds us hostage. Our choice is significant. Wholehearted obedience to God means liberty for us. His way is meant for our present fulfillment, happiness, and holiness. We are also rewarded with right standing in Him and eternal life. The only result of slavery to self and to sin is death.

DAY 1

"To God's elect, strangers in the world, . . . who have been chosen according to the foreknowledge of God the Father, through the sanctifying work of the Spirit, for obedience to Jesus Christ and sprinkling by his blood" (1 Pet. 1:1-2).

Believers are chosen by the Father, set apart by the Spirit, to obey Christ. Obedience is the very purpose of our sanctification. It results in spiritual blessing and peace as we enjoy freedom from the fears and controlling passions of sin.

The result of self-rule is fear and cowardice. But when God rules our life we have power and the peace of self-control. Disciplining self is a fruit of the Spirit's work in us.

Do you realize that you were elected by God for freedom? What evidence do you see of God's control in your life? Do you demonstrate that proof to those you lead?

Prayer: Dear Lord, thank You for choosing me. Guide me to be an obedient servant, an example to those who look to me for leadership.

DAY 2

"For we know that our old self was crucified with him so that the body of sin might be rendered powerless, that we should no longer be slaves to sin—because anyone who has died has been freed from sin" (Rom. 6:6-7).

When we identify with Christ's death, we are free from the control of sin. The old self is buried, and we have new life in Christ. This process requires our cooperation. First, we consider ourselves dead to sin, but alive to God. We don't let sin rule us anymore. Then, we continue to yield ourselves to God to carry out His righteousness. That's where we find our freedom and fulfillment and bring glory to Christ.

Have you considered yourself alive to God? Have you offered yourself to Him as a servant of righteousness?

Prayer: Christ, You have conquered death so that we may have life in You. Teach us, Lord, to consider ourselves dead to sin. We want to glorify You.

DAY 3

"I have been crucified with Christ and I no longer live, but Christ lives in me. The life I live in the body, I live by faith in the Son of God, who loved me and gave himself for me" (Gal. 2:20).

Once we die to our old life, Christ comes to live in us. We live our new life by relying on Him in complete trust. Christ empowers and completes us, so we can do the Father's will, serving Him in righteousness.

If we are truly Christ's disciples, we must totally give up our self-life to Him. That means denying our own interests and following Him in complete trust. We are to conform to His example in living and, if need be, in dying also. For Christ was servant to all, giving up Himself that we might live.

Has your old life been crucified? Are you relying on Christ in your new life?

Prayer: Gracious Father, thank You for the new life You have extended to me through Jesus Christ. Help me to be an example of His love to all I serve.

DAY 4

"Do not conform any longer to the pattern of this world, but be transformed by the renewing of your mind. Then you will be able to test and prove what God's will is—His good, pleasing and perfect will" (Rom. 12:2).

Spiritual battles are won or lost in our minds. The apostle Paul tells us that when we are *in* Christ, we have the mind of Christ. Here in Romans we see that change begins with a new attitude.

First, as believers we are not to conform (adapt) to the world and its superficial customs and values. Then, transformation occurs when our mind is renewed. The result is that, by example, we prove God's will is good and perfect, and by His grace we can perceive it. A disciplined mind brings freedom. Are there still ways you are conformed to this world's ideals? Are you able to discern God's will for your life?

Prayer: Lord, I want to know Your perfect will. Transform me—set me free from the world's patterns.

DAY 5

"Therefore, prepare your minds for action; be self-controlled; set your hope fully on the grace to be given you when Jesus Christ is revealed" (1 Pet. 1:13).

Because we have been raised to a new life in Christ, we can keep our minds set on higher things—the things that are above earthly values.

Hidden in Christ we have died to this world. This death is protection from the anger of God against sin. A mind kept on Christ has righteousness and peace.

As Christian leaders, we are spiritual warriors. Our minds must be braced and alert, ready for inevitable battles. Trusting the Holy Spirit to control self and set our hope unchangeably on God's divine favor, we will have the victory. Where is your mind set? Are you prepared for action? Have you died to self-interest?

Prayer: Gracious Lord, take control of my mind and set my mind on the hope and trust found only in You.

DAY 6

"Teach us to number our days aright, that we may gain a heart for wisdom" (Ps. 90:12).

Our days are truly short, but few of us live in that truth. If we could understand the brevity of our lives, we would make each day count for righteousness and we would number our days by our obedience, our acts of love to those we lead to peace in Christ, and by our hope for coming grace.

Disciplining our time becomes an act of worship. We live each minute aware of His presence, seeking to please Him and do His will, not our own. As disciplined Christian leaders, we recognize that we must be about the Father's business, reflecting Jesus' light to the world.

How do you count your days? Have you gained the wisdom needed?

Prayer: Father, You determine each day of our lives. Teach us to make each one count in light of eternity. We give them all to You.

DAY 7

"Whatever you do, work at it with all your heart, as working for the Lord, not for men, since you know that you will receive an inheritance from the Lord as a reward. It is the Lord Christ you are serving" (Col. 3:23-24).

Our focus in ministry must be to please Christ, not men. As this verse points out, He is the one who rewards us for our work. And the quality of our performance should be determined from the same perspective. No matter what the task, we should consider it a sacred act of worship performed not in our power but through the power of the Holy Spirit.

Do you always do your best work? How do you evaluate the tasks you've been given to do?

Prayer: Dear Lord, what a blessing to go about my work with dedication and interest knowing that it is done for You and not for my own gratification or the praise of others. Thank You that You alone give me the power to complete it and apart from you I can do nothing (John 15:5).

FOR FURTHER REFLECTION

1. A woman must develop and maintain a self-controlled life-style to implement her capabilities and reach personal goals. Write a definition of "self-control" based on the following verses:

> Proverbs 25:28; Acts 24:25; Galatians 5:23;
> 2 Peter 1:5-6.

a. Controlling our own desires and ordering our priorities and time according to God's direction creates discipline in our life. Write phrases that describe discipline in the verses below.

> Psalm 94:12-13; Proverbs 1:1-7; 5:23; 6:23; 10:17;
> 12:1; Hebrews 12:11; Revelation 3:19-22

b. Do you lead a disciplined and self-controlled life-style? List elements in your life that reflect these qualities.

2. How can you help those you lead develop discipline and self-control? Write five ways to do so here.

3. A disciplined, self-controlled life-style is reflected in the way we use our time. How do you spend your time? Copy the weekly schedule you developed with chapter 2 and put time allowance beside each activity.

a. How does your schedule reflect discipline in your life?

b. What is the ratio of time spent doing those things Go⌐ ꞌ to do in comparison to personal preference leisur⌐

*As you apply the principles of Elisabeth Elliot's essay to your life,
consider the following—L.M.*

PRICELESS BANK ACCOUNT

If you had a bank that credited your account each morning
with $86,400 but carried over no balance from day to day,
and allowed you to keep no cash in your account,
and every evening canceled the amount you had failed
to use during the day,
What would you do?
Draw out every cent, of course!

Well, you have such a bank, and its name is "TIME."
Every morning it credits you with 86,400 seconds.
Every night it rules off, as lost, whatever of this
you have failed to invest for a good purpose.
It carries over no balances. It allows no overdrafts.
Each day it opens a new account for you.
Each night it burns the records of that day.
If you fail to use the day's deposits, the loss is yours.
There is no drawing against the "tomorrow."
You must live in the present—on today's deposits.
Invest it so as to get from it the utmost in
health, happiness and success!

—Author Unknown

NOTES

[1]Ruth Ann Ridley, "Priority Living: Making Your Time Count," *Discipleship Journal*, Volume 25, 1985, 41.

[2]Excerpts from Elisabeth Elliot's, *Discipline, the Glad Surrender,* (Fleming H. Revell), used with the author's permission.

Corrie ten Boom writes, "A woodpecker tapped against the stem of a tree just as lightning struck the tree and destroyed it. He flew away and said, 'I didn't know there was so much power in my beak.' When we bring the Gospel there is a danger that we will think or say, 'I have done a good job.' Don't be a silly woodpecker. Know where your strength comes from. It is only the Holy Spirit who can make a message good and fruitful."[1]

Humility is a much needed but rarely found commodity in our society today. True humility stems from an understanding that though God gives a woman gifts and abilities in the area of leadership, they are of no greater or lesser value than the gifts He has given each member of His body. All are a result of God's power at work. We can take no credit.

Humility results from knowing that success flows directly from the Holy Spirit. Jesus declares this fact in John 15, "If a man remains in me and I in him, he will bear much fruit; apart from me you can do nothing" (v. 5).

With this understanding, Christian leaders are able to stand humbly before God and others, recognizing the source of all they are, have, and do. We each stand at the feet of Jesus, seeking to be obedient to the will of God.

How can you exemplify an attitude of humility? As you read the following essay, ask God to reveal areas of pride in your life which could be hindering your ministry and leadership. Search for new opportunities to surrender self-promotion and acknowledge His overwhelming grace at work in daily life.

—*L. R. M.*

CHAPTER 10

DEVELOPING A HUMBLE HEART

Fran Caffey Sandin

Fran Caffey Sandin, author of *See You Later, Jeffrey* and many articles, is a registered nurse, church organist, and Bible class leader. She is listed in Who's Who in American Colleges and Universities and Notable Women of Texas. Wife of urologist Dr. James Sandin, Fran has a daughter, Angie, and son, Steve, who live at home.

High above the white stone palace a colorful flag swayed gently in the breeze. On the pavement below, prancing horses led the brigade. Solemn-faced soldiers marched in perfect rows, their red uniforms and black plumed hats glistening in the warm summer sun. Our toes tapped to the thump of rhythmic bass drums. Their cadence echoed, then faded in the distance. Where was my family standing? Just outside the gates of Buckingham Palace.

Royalty. How awesome! The queen was at home. My heart pounded as I watched her protectors ceremoniously change guards. Now I understood why London commoners sought a glimpse of the queen, one of the wealthiest women in the world.

Is it possible that someone with an exalted position can also be humble? According to the following story, the answer is "yes."

"The late Queen Mary visited a hospital ward one day and paused for a moment at the bed of a little girl. She asked the child where she lived and the child answered 'Battersea,' a poor district of London.

'Where do you live?' the girl asked, unaware of the rank of the visitor.

'Oh, just behind Gorringe's department store,' Queen Mary replied.'"[2]

Queen Mary's graciousness illustrates a humble spirit. The queen did not pull rank. We have many avenues of influence. However, maintaining a spirit of humility may be our greatest challenge.

Who has not felt the "headiness" of opportunities such as chairing a prominent committee, speaking for a women's conference, or having something published? Have we not felt tempted to want others to serve us? Have we, at times, thought more highly of ourselves than we ought? Have we stubbornly balked at submission?

Karen Mains in her award-winning book, *With My Whole Heart,* observes: "We are so capable of corruption that even our service for God can become a source for pride. We need to learn to allow Christ to help us keep our fists tightly clenched upon humility."[3]

Many of us would agree that in our world of self-exaltation, pride is a nagging stumbling block. Scripture warns us that "Pride goes before destruction, a haughty spirit before a fall" (Prov. 16:18). It also reminds us that "Before his downfall a man's heart is proud, but humility comes before honor" (Prov. 18:12). How can we grasp the meaning of true humility and implement it in our lives?

Perhaps we gain some perspective by reviewing our common dilemma. Unfortunately, pride is at the core of our human natures. Just as we inherited this sin from our earthly father, Adam, we learn that biblical humility is impossible apart from the indwelling presence of Christ. He is our example.

Do nothing out of selfish ambition or vain conceit, but in humility consider others better than yourselves. Each of you should look not only to your own interests, but also to the interests of others.

Your attitude should be the same as that of Christ Jesus:

Who, being in very nature God, did not consider equality with God something to be grasped, but made himself nothing, taking the very nature of a servant, being made in human likeness. And being found in appearance as a man, he humbled himself and became obedient to death—even death on a cross! Therefore God exalted him to the highest place and gave him the name that is above every name, that at the name of Jesus every knee should bow, in heaven and on earth and under the earth, and every tongue confess that Jesus Christ is Lord, to the glory of God the Father. (Phil. 2:3-11)

"Humility was not considered a virtue in early days. Since no Greek or Latin words described humility prior to Christ's coming, He introduced a revolutionary concept His disciples found perplexing."[4] We have the same difficulty today. Christ's attitude of humility is just the opposite of our natural bent to selfishness and worldly self-indulgence.

In Matthew 11:29 Jesus says, "I am meek and lowly in heart" (KJV). J. Oswald Sanders in his book, *The Incomparable Christ*, writes, "Meekness plus lowliness constitutes humility. Meekness is humility in relation to God. Lowliness is humility in relation to man."[5]

The words *meekness* and *lowliness* do not imply becoming a doormat with eyes constantly lowered or dressing in rags. Nor do they suggest weakness or a sense of being inferior. Both meekness and lowliness denote humility and courtesy.

Are self-respect and self-worth being attacked in this verse? Not at all. Marge Caldwell, popular speaker and charm and modeling teacher, writes in *The Radiant You*:

> Respect yourself. If you have no self-respect, you can't expect others to respect you. Love yourself! Oh, I don't mean that kind of person with 'I' trouble. You know, "I, I, I" all the time.
>
> Jesus tells us to love our neighbor as we love ourselves. We have to live with ourselves all the time, and if we begin to hate ourselves and belittle ourselves constantly, we will lose self-respect. Humility is not in degrading yourself; it is in forgetting yourself.[6]

Meekness has been described as strength under control. Jesus was both strong in character and tenderhearted. His gentleness was manifested as He moved about unpretentiously among the common folk. For Christ humility was a choice, just as it is for us today. He totally submitted Himself to the Father's will. He gave us many reminders:

➤ "Blessed are the poor in spirit" (Matt. 5:3).
➤ "Blessed are the meek" (Matt. 5:5).
➤ "Therefore, whoever humbles himself like this child is the greatest in the kingdom of heaven" (Matt. 18:4).
➤ "For everyone who exalts himself will be humbled, and he who humbles himself will be exalted" (Luke 14:11).

➤ "He who is least among you all—he is the greatest" (Luke 9:48).

J. Oswald Sanders writes, "To read these passages thoughtfully is to be convicted of our lack of humility. Our pride stands abashed in the presence of His utter humility. One fact stands out crystal clear—God's way up is down."[7]

The following concepts may help us to develop a humble heart:

GRACE

"For it is by grace you have been saved, through faith—and this not from yourselves, it is the gift of God—not by works, so that no one can boast. For we are God's workmanship, created in Christ Jesus to do good works, which God prepared in advance for us to do" (Eph. 2:8-10).

One evening in 1971, my husband and I attended an evangelistic meeting. Since we were active church members I never dreamed that my life would be changed.

The pastor's message? "The Prodigal Son." How many times had I heard the story? That night, I'm ashamed to admit, I snuggled down in my seat, ready to "tune out" mentally and begin preparing the next day's shopping list.

But God had other plans. The stirring message vividly portrayed God's character as the prodigal's father watched from afar, yearning for the return of his willful, prideful, wayward son.

As I listened, I began to identity with the son's attitude, to recognize my own self-centeredness and pride. My soul was laid bare. Had I been in the far country and not known it? Suddenly I was walking beside the prodigal son, repenting, and rushing into the arms of our loving Father.

How patient He had been! Later at home, I mentally drew a picture of an altar. I imagined myself lying upon it; I asked God to take my life—body, soul, and spirit—that I might wholeheartedly glorify Him.

I whispered, "Jesus, in the past, I've had all of You, but You didn't have all of me. Tonight I give my life to You. I do not deserve Your forgiveness. I am unworthy of Your grace and love, but I thank You."

Joyfully I received the peace that passes understanding. Yes, my Father had been waiting to teach me many things. At last I had a teachable spirit.

The brokenness I felt was accompanied by new freedom and power. I knew that regardless of the task I encountered, it was no longer necessary to seek approval of men. I was accountable to God.

The seed of humility is planted in each of our hearts the moment we recognize two things: the righteousness and holiness of God, and our bankruptcy without Christ. To swallow our pride is a bitter decision, but by doing it we take the first step toward becoming an instrument in God's hands.

To grow in grace and Christ-awareness we can:

➤ Be faithful in daily Bible study and prayer.

➤ Read books that describe the attributes and character of God.

➤ Study the lives of great men and women of faith and prayer.

➤ Plan times of fasting ("I humbled my soul with fasting," Ps. 35:13, NASB).

➤ Ask the Holy Spirit to help make us more sensitive to His leading.

We can ask:

➤ Am I self-centered or Christ-centered?

➤ Do I have a teachable spirit? Am I thoughtful and kind?

➤ Am I willing to acknowledge that, apart from God's grace, I would not have life and purpose?

➤ Am I jealous of others and their talents, or do I view each individual as gifted by God's sovereign grace?

GRACIOUSNESS

The telephone rang at my home one day with a surprising call. It was a representative from WMBI, a Christian radio station in Chicago, calling to request an interview concerning one of my magazine articles.

If I had been gracious, I would have thanked her and simply made the arrangements. However, pride crept into our conversation as I asked if she knew about my book. I felt so important! That moment of self-promotion led to an icy response from the caller. The result? She said she would contact me later. She never did. Had I been graceful in speaking about the article, she probably would have asked me about the book. Unfortunately, I lost the opportunity for both. In short, I blew it.

A gracious woman could be described as gentle, courteous, tactful, kind, thoughtful, pleasant, friendly, and eager to help others.

A good self-image is an important element in humility. It gives us a more matter-of-fact approach to life's situations. We can more easily admit our errors and ask forgiveness.

When we are identified with Christ, our self-esteem is secure in His acceptance and unconditional love. As a result, we become more mature. We are freed from the bondage of constantly needing our emotional batteries charged by the approval of others.

The late Mary C. Crowley was truly a gracious woman. As one of the most successful business people in the nation, her aim was to help women become all that God meant them to be. "I believe in the dignity and importance of women," she said with a slight Southern drawl. "God doesn't take time to make a nobody."

In twenty-seven years, her Home Interiors and Gifts company grew from a $6,000 initial bank loan to $400 million in yearly sales. Mary was generous with her staff, but she gave them more than income. She guided them spiritually, helped them gain self-confidence and God-confidence. She stated, "When we see what it costs Jesus to redeem us, then somehow we take on a better self-image. Our self-image is then tied up in the character of God."[8] Mary did not keep treasures of wisdom to herself. Graciously, she shared them with others and in doing so pointed them to the Savior whom she dearly loved.

To become more gracious we can ask these questions:

> ➤ Am I tactful? Before speaking, do I consider the impact my words will have on the feelings of others?
> ➤ When I walk into a room am I thinking, *Here I am* or *There you are?*
> ➤ Do I control and manipulate others to get my own way?
> ➤ Am I quarrelsome?
> ➤ Do I become defensive or easily lose my temper?
> ➤ Am I willing to ask forgiveness when I am wrong?

First Peter 5:5-7 says, "Young men, in the same way be submissive to those who are older. Clothe yourselves with humility toward one another, because 'God opposes the proud but gives grace to the humble' [see Prov. 3:34]. Humble yourselves, therefore, under God's mighty hand, that he may lift you up in due time. Cast all your anxiety on him because he cares for you."

Giving

When placed in a position of leadership, we shouldn't rush to reserve a room in the ivory tower. Serving is our goal, not recognition. Christ seemed to know that descriptive words alone would not be enough to help us understand serving. He taught by example.

One of the most poignant scenes takes place at the Lord's Supper. The disciples began arguing and quarreling over who would be the greatest in Christ's kingdom (Luke 22:24). Sound familiar? When they arrived at a private home, to avoid danger and to secretly eat in the upstairs room, no slave was available to wash the disciples' feet as was customary in those days. Since no one offered to take on this menial task, Jesus stood, took a towel and basin, and washed the disciples' feet (John 13:1-15). By doing this, the Lord graphically demonstrated the essence of humility.

Humility means we are willing to follow His example, to do the lowly task, to set the table, or clean up after speaking at the banquet. It is an attitude of the heart. Giving and serving go hand in hand.

Charles Swindoll writes, "Nothing is more refreshing than a servant's heart and a giving spirit, especially when we see them displayed in a person many would tag as a celebrity." He describes meeting Colonel James B. Irwin, former astronaut who had made a successful moon walk.

Irwin told about his thrilling mission. "And then," Swindoll writes, "he began to realize en route back home that many would consider him a 'superstar' for sure, an international celebrity.

"Humbled by the awesome goodness of God, Colonel Irwin shared his true feelings, which went something like this:

"'As I was returning to earth, I realized that I was a servant—not a celebrity. So I am here as God's servant on planet Earth to share what I have experienced that others might know the glory of God.'"[9]

Swindoll adds a couple of revealing tests of humility:

1. A nondefensive spirit when confronted. This reveals a willingness to be accountable. Genuine humility operates on a rather simple philosophy. Nothing to prove, nothing to lose.

2. An authentic desire to help others. I'm referring to a sensitive, spontaneous awareness of needs. A true servant stays in touch with the

struggles others experience. There is that humility of mind that continually looks for ways to serve and to give.[10]

A true servant is "real." As true servants, we are free to admit failure because we know that failure is part of our human condition. When we are transparent and honest, others will want to hear what we have to say. If we pretend perfection or seem to "have all the answers," our audience disappears.

Another aspect of servanthood is the concept of evaluating and understanding ourselves. Both our talents and temperaments are God-given. When taken to extremes, at times our strengths can become weaknesses. For example, a person with strong leadership abilities may become bossy. Someone with peacemaking skills may dodge loving confrontation when it is needed.

Thus, humility involves an accurate assessment of our abilities, not to overestimate or underestimate ourselves, as we bring our total being under the Holy Spirit's control.

Serving, by definition, implies submission. A number of biblical examples come to mind, but one of the greatest is John the Baptist. He continually pointed to Jesus and said, "He must become greater; I must become less" (John 3:30). As leader, our goal is the same.

Christ's humility is most strikingly demonstrated through His response to suffering, insult, and character assassination. Through it all, even while bleeding on Calvary, Jesus never verbalized bitterness, self-justification, or complaint. If we are to be effective leaders, we cannot hold grudges or harbor ill will. Forgiveness is a choice. Because Jesus chose to forgive when we were undeserving, we can forgive others who offend us.

To enhance our serving spirit, we can ask:

➢ How do I care for those around me?

➢ Am I obedient to God?

➢ Does someone need my forgiveness? Do I need to forgive someone who has offended me?

GRATEFULNESS

My Grandpa Speights was a Scotch-Irish farmer. He depended upon the Lord for everything. He knew what it meant to pray literally for daily bread. One of the most outstanding characteristics I remember about him was his earnest mealtime prayer, "Lord, give us grateful hearts for these and all your many blessings."

Those words have been ingrained in my thought since childhood. However, through the years I've learned that gratefulness is another virtue that does not come naturally.

We've all heard of the "self-made" man who supposedly yanked himself up by his bootstraps. With adversity hanging on his back, he climbed the ladder of success by himself. Myth! Taking all the credit for our accomplishments, whatever they may be, is short-sighted and ungrateful.

In Luke 17, Jesus was approached by ten lepers. "'Jesus, Master, have pity on us!' When he saw them, he said, 'Go, show yourselves to the priests.' And as they went, they were cleansed. One of them, when he saw he was healed, came back, praising God in a loud voice. He threw himself at Jesus' feet and thanked Him—[even though] he was a Samaritan.

"Jesus asked, 'Were not all ten cleansed? Where are the other nine? Was no one found to return and give praise to God except this foreigner?' Then he said to him, 'Rise and go; your faith has made you well'" (vv. 10-19). The leper who returned was rewarded by learning that his faith played a part in his healing. Also his spirit of gratefulness pleased the Lord.

Humility and gratefulness are companions. As we stop to count our blessings, we realize that all are from God's hand. We can say with David, "Who am I, O Sovereign Lord, and what is my family, that you have brought me this far?" (2 Sam. 7:18).

Expressing gratefulness to one another is not only a common courtesy, but a spiritual encouragement. Receiving a compliment with a gracious "thank you" is all that is needed. If we apologize or dismiss the compliment, we sadly reject a pretty package of words. If we think of compliments as love gifts, they will brighten any day.

Gratefulness to God deepens as we walk through life's valleys and find Him in the dark. It's easy to praise God and be grateful when things are going well. However, when we are hurting, thankfulness and praise become an act of the will, not the emotions. As Christ carries us through pain, we have an opportunity to increase our humility by empathizing with others who suffer.

To develop a more grateful spirit, we can:

➤ List our blessings and thank God for them.

➤ Think about people who've influenced us; write and thank them for their contribution to our lives.

➤ Practice saying "thank you" often, especially at home.

Paul reminds us in Galatians 5:22-23, 25-26, "The fruit of the Spirit is love, joy, peace, patience, kindness, goodness, faithfulness, gentleness and self-control. Since we live by the Spirit, let us keep in step with the Spirit. Let us not become conceited, provoking and envying each other."

Developing a humble heart is an ongoing process, an out-growth of a Spirit-filled life. By seeking and feeding our natural desires, pride reigns in our life. But if we stay closely identified with Christ and His purposes, humility will emanate from our hearts, bringing glory and honor to our King. Charles Haddon Spurgeon encourages us by writing: "Humility is the acceptance of the place appointed by God, whether it be in the front or in the rear. God will deny no blessing to a thoroughly humbled spirit."[11]

THOUGHTS FOR DAILY MEDITATION

"Who has saved us and called us to a holy life—not because of anything we have done but because of his own purpose and grace. This grace was given us in Christ Jesus before the beginning of time" (2 Tim. 1:9-10).

Grace is a gift, not to be earned, but freely given by God. He gives it through Christ to reveal His love to us and to further His plans. Jesus is God's gift of grace made real. It is God's redemptive mercy set in contrast to our empty works and striving to fulfill the law. We could never meet God's standard of holiness and perfection, so He sent His Son to die for our sin and replaced our failed record with Christ's perfect record of righteousness. Amazing grace is that when God sees us, He sees His Son.

He has called us to holiness—a life set apart to serve Him. Through His favor we discover the Holy Spirit's power and equipment to pass on the gift of grace to others. As grace works in us we grow in His love. We are then enabled to display God's character through our lives.

A humble heart is the natural result of seeing God's grace actively at work in our lives. The Spirit works without our effort and sometimes in spite of it. Gratitude comes when we realize that even when we fail and fall short of God's glory, His grace overcomes our lack with his abundance. A humble heart is the only response.

Day 1

"But to each one of us grace has been given as Christ apportioned it" (Eph. 4:7).

Grace is the power of the Holy Spirit at work in our lives. James tells us we can receive more and more of this power as we humble ourselves (Jas 4:6). Although God continually makes His grace available, those who are haughty and self-important cannot receive it. They depend on themselves and their resources—missing the grace God offers.

We learn that Jesus Christ Himself assigns the gift of grace to each of us. In His eyes we are individuals separate and distinct. Knowing us intimately, He wisely chooses the measure of grace we need.

Do you recognize Christ's personal love for you? Are you growing in it?

Prayer: Thank You, Lord Jesus, for seeing me as I am and in spite of my faults and failures, offering me the glorious gift of grace.

Day 2

"But grow in the grace and knowledge of our Lord and Savior Jesus Christ" (2 Pet. 3:18).

Increase in our spiritual power is a growth process. We grow in grace as we yield to and depend on Christ's Holy Spirit. So we need to search for, recognize, and understand the person of our Lord and Savior, Jesus Christ. As our knowledge of Him increases, concentration on our own desires diminishes, releasing His power to work His grace in our hearts.

Do you know Christ as Lord and Savior? Does your life reflect growth in grace?

Prayer: Heavenly Father, help me to know You better, desire Your will and give You glory for the work of Your grace in and through my life.

Day 3

"The Lord is gracious and compassionate, slow to anger and rich in love" (Ps. 145:8).

God's goodness, kindness, and tenderness are expressed in graciousness. They are seen as attributes of His character through His action of righteousness, patience, and compassion. Repeatedly in Scripture we see God's graciousness toward His people and all others. He deals tenderly with us, providing all we need to accomplish His will for our lives and to fulfill our joy. God abounds in mercy. His love is rich.

Most of us have both bright and dark days. At times we may think the dark ones prevail. Even so, if we act with grace and justice, remembering our Savior and Lord, light shines even in the dark times of trial, sorrow, and doubt. What better motivation could there be for choosing the "right" road?

Are you gracious even on your darkest days? Are you tenderhearted and gracious toward others?

Prayer: Gracious God, thank You for being with me at all times. Your goodness is overwhelming.

Day 4

"You, my brothers, were called to be free. But do not use your freedom to indulge the sinful nature; rather serve one another in love. The entire law is summed up in a single command: 'Love your neighbor as yourself'" (Gal. 5:13-14).

Christ's death released us from the law. We no longer serve out of duty or obligation, but because of love. The Spirit prompts us to acts of love which bring life to others. This new way brings fulfillment and great joy as we serve others.

Perhaps the greatest proof of our humility is our servanthood. The freedom we have in Christ is not meant for self-indulgence. On the contrary. We have the unique opportunity to fulfill all the law by simply loving others. That love is demonstrated in acts of service as a tangible means to express our Christian love.

Do you love others as you do yourself? Are you leading them in love?

Prayer: Holy Spirit, I wait for Your prompting so that I may serve others with love.

DAY 5

"It is the Lord Christ you are serving" (Col. 3:24).

Our readiness to serve will be rewarded by Christ Himself. We are to know with certainty it is Christ we serve and not men. We serve Christ; therefore, we should not seek praise or reward from those we serve. Christ will reward us. He is the One we are to love and obey in our service to others. When we are obedient to His plan, He provides all we need to carry it out. Who are you serving? The Lord? Do you depend on Him for the strength you need to do your work?

Prayer: Lord Jesus, grant me the knowledge of Your desire for my work, the skill to accomplish it, and the strength to finish it.

DAY 6

"Enter his gates with thanksgiving and his courts with praise; give thanks to him and praise his name" (Ps. 100:4).

Praise and thanksgiving are avenues into God's courts. Throughout the Old Testament we see the priests' main function as leading the people in praise to God with thankfulness. Prayers and praise were the keys that preceded battles and demonstrations of God's powers.

The Amplified Bible says, "Let them sacrifice the sacrifices of thanksgiving, and rehearse His deeds with shouts of joy and singing" (Ps. 107:22). Thanksgiving is not always one of our spontaneous tendencies. More often it's a sacrifice. But when we consider His unfailing love and His wonderful deeds we should delight in singing His praises.

Do you recall God's wonderful deeds? Have you praised Him and thanked Him before making your requests? Are you grateful?

Prayer: Dear Lord, show me Your way and remind me to be thankful for the blessings You alone have and will grant. It is in viewing Your gifts with gratitude that I am humbled.

DAY 7

"But we ought always to thank God for you, brothers loved by the Lord, because from the beginning God chose you to be saved by the sanctifying work of the Spirit and through belief in the truth" (2 Thess. 2:13).

According to Paul, we should always be thankful to God for our work, for the ones He has placed under our leadership. Just think, they were chosen as His beloved children for sanctification. He has a grand plan for their lives and has given us the privilege of having a part in encouraging that plan to unfold. What a privilege—and obligation!

Prayer: Heavenly Father, grant me the insight to see the value in those I lead and to recognize that You have a plan for each life.

FOR FURTHER REFLECTION

1. Humility is of great value in God's sight. He will do whatever is necessary to bring us to the point of being humble so that He can use us. Read Numbers 12:3; Psalm 18:27; and Deuteronomy 8:2,16 to learn of God's work of humility.

a. Read the following verses and write phrases that tell of God's response to a heart that is humble.

Psalm 25:9; Proverbs 3:3-4; Isaiah 66:2

b. What do you learn from Matthew 11:29 and Philippians 2:5-11 about Jesus' attitude of humility?

2. Clear guidelines are given in the New Testament concerning an attitude of humility. What do you learn from the following verses?

Ephesians 4:2; James 4:10; 1 Peter 3:8; 5:6

3. Describe ways you can help those you lead develop an attitude of humility.

NOTES

[1]Corrie ten Boom, *Clippings from My Notebook* (World Wide Publishing, 1984), 56.

[2]Eleanor Doan, *The New Speaker's Sourcebook* (Grand Rapids, Mich.: Zondervan Publishing House, 1968), 209.

[3]Karen Burton Mains, *With My Whole Heart* (Portland, Ore.: Multnomah Press, 1987), 121.

[4]J. Oswald Sanders, *The Incomparable Christ* (Chicago: Moody Press, 1971), 110.

[5]Ibid.

[6]Marge Caldwell, *The Radiant You* (self-published, printed in the USA, 1968), 25.

[7]Sanders, 113.

[8]Pat Assimakopoulos, "Mary C. Crowley Believes in Women," *The Christian Writer*, December 1985, 13-16.

[9]Charles Swindoll, *Improving Your Serve* (Waco,Tex.: Word Incorporated, 1981), 18-19.

[10]Ibid., 25.

[11]Doan, 210.

As each character quality is developed, clear communication remains the essential bridge to influencing those we lead. Our communication, both verbal and nonverbal, projects the final message.

In *Leadership Is an Art*, Max DePree explains that communication performs two functions: educating and liberating. *Educate* comes from two Latin words that mean "to lead or draw out."[1] How we lead or draw out others in response to our message depends on our ability to communicate.

How well do you communicate? Do others respond warmly to your conversation as if you have reached out to embrace them or does a cold, stiff manner leave them feeling somehow rejected? What does your body language communicate? Do you seem closed or open to discussion? Are you interested and concerned?

Have you honed your listening skills? As you reflect on Annie Chapman's thoughts, ask the Holy Spirit to convict you of ways you communicate attitudes unacceptable to a life possessed by Christ. Pray for greater sensitivity to the Holy Spirit and the needs of those to whom God has called you to minister.

Select specific ways you can develop more effective methods of communication as a Christian leader. The results will be liberating.

—L. R. M.

CHAPTER 11

COMMUNICATING WITH CLARITY

Annie Chapman

Annie Chapman is a Christian songwriter, author, wife, and mother who performs nationwide with her husband, Steve. Recording for more than ten years, the Chapmans have recorded ten albums. Their music and message on the family has been featured in numerous Christian magazines. Her latest and third book, *Smart Women Keep It Simple,* is an inside look at her personal journey, which hasn't always been simple.

In the corner of our simple den is a machine that represents just how far we've come in our ability to communicate with the world around us. This device looks like a regular telephone, but in fact it is one unit that has three incredible functions. With the touch of a few buttons, I can talk clearly to my mother some four hundred miles away. When I'm not home, this same machine will speak for me in my absence.

Even more amazing, I can send a written message across the telephone wires, and it will be received on the other end without even wrinkling the paper.

Do I understand even a small part of this communication device? Absolutely not! Instead of "user friendly," the manual should have said "idiot tolerant." Even though I have no earthly idea how it works, I know that it does.

The same is true when it comes to communicating effectively the message of Christ. Though I don't understand fully how this message of hope and redemption can change and transform a life, I know it does. In John 12:32, we read that Jesus said, "If I be lifted up from the earth, [I] will draw all men unto me" (KJV). So the ultimate purpose of communication is to lift Christ up as the answer to all questions and all needs.

133

Realizing the life-altering ability of the message of Christ when it is successfully channeled through the process of communication, I continue to use it and seek to use it more effectively.

Communication has several facets. Each part is necessary in order to accomplish the stated goal of sharing Christ with a world in need.

COMMUNICATING THROUGH UNDERSTANDING

One night after our concert a middle-aged, overweight, rather poorly kept woman walked over to talk. I could tell she'd been crying as she poured out her sad story.

One year earlier her fifteen-year-old son had been brutally murdered by a gang of teenagers. Now, her twelve-year-old daughter was talking of suicide because she wanted to go be with her brother.

Finding little help from her withdrawn, nonbelieving husband, she reached out to her local church, only to find that the small rural congregation had little or no resources to help her cope or to help her daughter avoid the tragedy of a suicidal attempt.

As the woman talked, I listened intently. The eye contact, body posture, facial expressions, and frequent nods would have appeared to any onlooker that communication was occurring. However, not until I put my arm around her and tenderly lifted up her request for help to the Lord did communication transpire. As we prayed and as her shoulders relaxed, I sensed her relief. She appreciated the fact that I cared about her and wanted to understand her pain.

This woman, and countless others, are looking for someone to offer words of solace and a heart of understanding. Colossians 4:6 says, "Let your speech be always with grace, seasoned with salt, that ye may know how ye ought to answer every man"(KJV). Once again I realized that though talking and listening are important components of the communication process, the cycle is not complete until an exchange of understanding is included.

On another occasion Steve and I were going to make a four-hour trip to the airport after a concert. Before we started the long trek, we changed from our concert outfits into jeans and sweatshirts, and I removed my makeup. We then stopped at a fast-food restaurant to grab a sandwich before leaving town. A woman who attended the concert came over to speak to me.

After complimenting the evening, she then said, "I wa
balcony and from a distance you look young and pretty,
see you up close, I see that you are neither."

Needing to respond but not wanting to say what I felt like saying
("May the fleas of a thousand camels invade your nostrils"), I tried to
be tactful but couldn't sincerely express thanks for such a comment.

After seventeen years of traveling I have developed some pretty thick
skin. I do admit, however, I thought fast to come up with a response to
this unsolicited critique of my appearance. I said, "That's a very interesting observation."

My reply apparently was not what she expected. Sensing that perhaps I had not heard her, she actually repeated her offensive comment
about me being old and ugly. This time I gave her what she apparently
wanted to hear. I said, "Thank you." At times like this Ephesians 4:29
comes to mind, or at least perhaps it should, "Let no corrupt communication proceed out of your mouth, but that which is good to the use
of edifying, that it may minister grace unto the hearers" (KJV).

Fully content that she had completed the communication process,
sensing that understanding had transpired, she returned to her table.

COMMUNICATING THROUGH APPEARANCE

My world view has been expanded through the marvelous experience of having teenagers in my home. With a son who is growing quite
proficient in the execution of the electric guitar (execution, now that's a
good idea), I have been introduced to the rather confusing world of
Christian "head-banger" music, and I use the word *music* loosely.

In all fairness, Nathan uses a good deal of wisdom when selecting his
music. But there is something I find interesting in regard to this particular style of music. The appearance of the people singing sometimes
communicates an even louder message than that which they sing and
speak. The medium becomes the message.

Maybe I'm showing my age, but when young men have hair down
to their rears, wear more makeup than I, and attire themselves in span-
dex jumpsuits that leave little to the imagination, while they squat and
scream Scripture verses, I get a mixed message. Communication is happening, but what I see speaks much louder than what I hear.

The concept of our appearance speaking louder than our words and thus limiting our message applies to more than rock bands. In the spring of 1988 I was asked to speak to a ladies' retreat for the Southeast Christian Church in Louisville, Kentucky, scheduled for the following March. Steve and I had been to the church in 1988 and so the people were familiar with me and my message.

While praying about what I should prepare to share (I was to speak for four one-hour presentations), I felt the Lord impress on me to share how He could change the things we hate most about ourselves. As I contemplated this subject matter, I argued with the Lord.

"Lord, I can't speak on that subject because I have never let you deal with the things that keep me back. I am unqualified."

I sensed His reply, "Well, we have a year to do that." I thought about Esther and how she was put on a twelve-month beauty regimen (Esth. 2:12). So, for the following twelve months I made a list of the things about myself that bothered me and thus limited the message of my life. I set out, with God's help, to change these things.

There were many things in my life that could not be seen that needed changing. For instance, I watched too much television. I needed to be more consistent in my prayer and Bible study. There was necessary work concerning my relationship with my children, such as the angry responses to childish behavior. And there was the deep feelings of inferiority (self-loathing) that caused me to push people back, rejecting them before they could reject me.

These problems were biggies for me to work on. There were also some outward things that needed to change. I've always had a weight problem, and so there was the issue of thirty-five extra pounds that needed to come off. I wanted to remove some moles. In fact, my entire appearance needed revamping since I hadn't changed my hair style in twenty years.

Well, 1988 became a life-changing year for me. When I arrived to share that weekend in 1989 I walked in and no one recognized me. The year before they saw a size fourteen plus, matronly woman, but the woman who showed up to speak a year later was a size six, confident person who knew that God could change a life.

Did these women listen when I spoke about God's ability to change us inside and out? The message they saw validated the message I spoke.

Not only does our appearance limit our ability to communicate our message, but the way we live can also hinder what needs to be communicated.

COMMUNICATING THROUGH BEHAVIOR

One day when I was in the midst of finishing up the final manuscript on the book, *Smart Women Keep It Simple*, the children came home from school. I met them at the door and stated in my Sergeant Chapman tone of voice, "I have to get this book done today. There will be no supper tonight. Don't talk to me. Don't ask me any questions. You'll just have to do the best you can."

Nathan, my perceptive and disgustingly honest teenaged son, said, "Just one question, Mom. What's the name of that book you're working on?"

Nailed! He nailed me dead to rights. I sheepishly confessed the book was about making our lives simple and in balance with godly priorities. He then went on to console my punctured heart by saying, "Mom, you're not really a hypocrite because before you started the book you really did have your priorities straight."

What would I do without my family to keep me honest? I pity those public people who don't have the advantage of brutally honest friends and family to pull them back and challenge them to line up their lives with the message they speak. There is nothing more tragic, it is said, than to be a "public success and a private failure." What our lives reveal is much more articulate than what we say.

By the way, I did cook dinner that night, and finish the book, too, but don't ask me if I felt smart at the end.

COMMUNICATING THROUGH LISTENING

One of the most overlooked elements of communication is listening. Fifteen times in the New Testament Christ admonishes, "He who has ears to hear, let him hear." This indicates that hearing involves more than just the physical ability to hear, but has more to do with listening to what is said.

In William Bachus' book, *Telling Each Other the Truth*, many suggestions are given to help facilitate listening. The practical techniques such as facing the speaker, making eye contact, nodding, altering facial expressions appropriately or perhaps saying "uh-huh" occasionally are suggested. He goes on to quote Dr. Val Arnold, a noted psychologist who offers the S-O-L-E-R plan for the key to invite another to listen.

Squarely face the other person

Open your body position by uncrossing legs and unfolding arms

Lean toward the other person

Eye contact should be made from time to time (not steady staring)

Relax and be comfortable.[2]

James 1:19 says, "Let every man [woman] be swift to hear, slow to speak, slow to wrath"(KJV). Using this guideline for communication, we then are instructed in verse 22 to "Be ye doers of the word, and not hearers only" (KJV). Listening opens up the way to know the right way to proceed. Effective listening is a communication skill worth learning, but it doesn't come naturally to many of us. Dr. Bachus suggests that what seems to be listening isn't listening at all.

Free Association—Hearing a portion of what the other speaker said, we allow ourselves the free liberty to take off and start thinking about something totally unrelated. This may lead to embarrassment when a response is expected to a specific point.

Piecemeal Listening—Some of us listen to a person, waiting and ready to pounce on a phrase or topic to which we feel sufficiently versed. Instead of hearing what this person is saying, we simply react from our vantage point.

Waiting to Argue—It's hard to listen to someone talk about a subject important to us, one about which we have a firmly established set of beliefs. Instead we become agitated; our eyes shift about while we wait for the speaker to take a breath. At the first opportunity we jump in and state our side of the argument. This may be a challenging form of debate for some, but it does not facilitate communication.

Killing Time—Some of us don't even try to listen. When put in a position where someone bent on talking corners us, we say little. To escape being a part of the conversation, we tend to take mental vacations, waiting for our chance to talk or to get away.

I see this noncommunicative form of listening happen at parties, business/social gatherings, or even after church services. If you are unfortunate enough to be the speaker, you may notice the unwilling listener looking around for someone more interesting or more often a "bigger dog" with whom they wish to be seen.

Listening to Judge—When talking and listening, sometimes we feel we are so intuitive that we are able to discern negative motives and thoughts. This can be a real problem when we place ourselves in the position of making mental evaluations of a situation about which we have little or perhaps biased information. This kind of listening may lead to many things, but true communication is not one of them.

As we women in ministry develop the ability to listen, it will greatly influence our sensitivity to the voice of the Holy Spirit speaking to our hearts and giving us that divine guidance that is essential in order to understand the person who's speaking to us. We desperately need discernment to know if all a person needs is a sincere listening ear, or if they need more concrete help and advice.

While ministering at a youth camp a few years ago, I went to the altar to pray with a young lady. As we talked with each other and with the Lord, she confessed that she had a terrible problem with sexual promiscuity. I asked her about her relationship with her father and she began to tell me through her tears that there had never been a loving relationship with her dad.

While we prayed the Lord spoke to me to comfort her. I told her that I sensed the Lord wanting her to know that He loved her and did not condemn her, that the void in her life could be filled if she allowed the heavenly Father to love her the way she had wanted her earthly father to love her.

Through the experience of hearing her confession and then hearing what God had to say about it, the song "Her Daddy's Love" was written. Communication took place as we spoke. I listened and then shared with her what I felt the Holy Spirit was saying. Since that time, the song's message has communicated God's love and forgiveness to countless fathers and daughters. This is communication in action.

COMMUNICATING WITHIN LIMITATIONS

Communication is not limited to the great orators whose command of the English language brings us to our feet with accolades of praise and action. Communication can and does occur through individuals with extreme limitations.

Helen Keller through a childhood disease at eighteen months of age was left blind, deaf, and mute. Left with so little faculties she would not be a person we would automatically put in the class of the "great communicators." Yet, despite, or perhaps because of her disabilities, she developed a "voice" that has been heard around the world.

The message that "God's strength is perfected in our weakness" is personified in this afflicted, yet remarkable woman. Although blind and deaf, she graduated *cum laude* from Radcliffe, authored seven books and countless articles, and traveled the continent educating people concerning the needs of the disabled. In poetry, she revealed she did not view her life as limited.

> They took away what should have been my eyes.
> *(But I remembered Milton's Paradise)*
> They took away what should have been my ears
> *(Beethoven came and wiped away my tears)*
> They took away what should have been my tongue.
> *(But I had talked with God when I was young)*
> He would not let them take away my soul.
> *(Possessing that I still possess the whole)*

The story is told of another unsung communicator whose limitations did not prevent her from fulfilling God's plan to communicate the good news. She was an old Russian woman who lay on a sofa, propped up with pillows to keep her body upright, a body twisted almost beyond recognition by multiple sclerosis.

Corrie ten Boom visited her, using the cover of darkness to escape detection by the Lithuanian authorities. When Corrie walked across the room and kissed the woman's wrinkled cheek, the elderly woman responded by rolling her eyes and smiling. The atrophied muscles in her neck would no longer allow her to move her head. She could control only her right hand. With little more than an index finger, this brave woman communicated the message of the gospel as she pecked out the letters on a battered typewriter. Using one finger she translated Christian books and portions of the Bible into Russian.[3]

Last July, Steve and his mom visited his granddad. Upon leaving, Steve's mom hugged him and said, "I love you, Dad." The old gentleman, who never communicated love verbally, uttered a weak, "uh-huh."

That was it. At ninety-six years he still struggled to express love and affection. Steve's mom wasn't put out by his lack of words. She looked at his hands and saw a finger missing on each hand. She remembered the steel pin in his hip and the black lung disease he had battled for years.

For over forty years, Ewing Steele worked the coal mines of West Virginia providing for eleven children and the woman he loved. Did he communicate love to his family? You bet he did. The following words were written to help express the fact that even in the absence of verbal expertise, communication can take place. The key is to learn to listen with senses other than hearing.

LOVE WAS SPOKEN
Before the sun came up, daddy rolled out of bed
He'd go to work, and that's how love was said.
He'd spend the money, that he made all week
To feed a hungry family, that's how love would speak.
Love was spoken, though daddy rarely used the words.
Love was spoken in everything he did, love was all we heard.
On Saturday morning, when a man ought to rest
Dad would work on the house, and that's how love was said.
When Sunday came, we were off to the chapel,
Love was spoken, so pure and simple.
Saying love did not come easy.
Though we did not criticize
But we could hear him say, "I love you"
When we listened with our eyes.
Love was spoken, though daddy never used the words
Love was spoken, in everything he did, love was all we heard.[4]

THOUGHTS FOR DAILY MEDITATION

For this reason he had to be made like his brothers in every way, in order that he might become a merciful and faithful high priest in service to God, and that he might make atonement for the sins of the people. Because he himself suffered when he was tempted, he is able to help those who are being tempted (Heb. 2:17-18).

Christ is our example in every aspect of leadership. This passage in Hebrews shows the extent to which Jesus went to communicate His understanding to man. Jesus, Lord of all, took on human nature. His role as merciful and faithful high priest required this complete identification. He faced the same temptations we face so He could understand and help us.

Empathy plays a powerful role in leadership. When we don't seek answers to the problems people face, when we don't listen with compassion and sympathy, we are displaying poor leadership qualities. Being heard and understood brings great comfort and relief in any situation.

DAY 1

"Praise be to the God and Father of our Lord Jesus Christ, the Father of compassion and the God of all comfort, who comforts us in all our troubles, so that we can comfort those in any trouble with the comfort we ourselves have received from God" (2 Cor. 1:3-4).

The comfort we've been given is meant to be passed on to others. God offers us compassion in all our trials. He knows how to comfort us.

Brotherly love, compassion, and sympathy identify believers. The Bible says that this is how the world will know we belong to God. These virtues also provide the environment we all need to mature in our Christian walk. Wise leaders establish and promote harmony. It makes their job easier.

How do you encourage harmony and understanding with those you lead? Does compassion mark your ministry?

Prayer: Gracious Father, grant me the gift of compassion as I plan and work with others. Help me to be in touch with their feelings and troubles.

DAY 2

"He is the image of the invisible God, the firstborn over all creation" (Col. 1:15).

The Amplified Bible says, "He is the exact likeness of the unseen God—the visible representation of the invisible." His appearance on earth was to reveal God to us, so we could be reconciled.

While we are not to judge by outward appearance alone, how we look represents who we belong to. Jesus appeared to make God real to men. Now we make Him visible to the world. Our countenance is a great testimony to our Owner. Do your eyes, expressions, and demeanor reflect Christ's tender kindness and compassion? Does your manner portray genuine concern? Do you shine with the love of God?

Prayer: Father, may every aspect of my life speak well of You to the world.

Day 3

"Do not lie to each other, since you have taken off your old self with its practices and have put on the new self, which is being renewed in knowledge in the image of its Creator" (Col. 3:9-10).

The frailty of our human vessels was meant to display the greatness of God's power. Our weakness reveals His precious treasure within. The weaker we are, the greater His power is shown.

Pretense means the false appearance of looking good. It is a practice of our old self. When we clothe ourselves with Christ, we no longer need to deceive each other. Our appearance will reflect our inner renewal as we become more and more like Him.

Have you seen your weakness display the greatness of God's power? Have you put on your new clothes in Christ?

Prayer: Lord Jesus, forgive my pretenses and help me to be more like You, without any effort to cover up my faults and weaknesses.

Day 4

"Set an example for the believers in speech, in life, in love, in faith and in purity" (1 Tim. 4:12).

Even though Timothy was a young believer, Paul admonished him to be an example in his behavior, thereby proving his maturity in the faith. Every aspect of our lives communicates to others who we really are—our words, our love and our purity can point to the reality of our relationship with God. Behavior can actually say more than our speech. It's the visual aid of our faith. Our conduct validates our beliefs.

What do your actions communicate about your faith? How does your behavior act as an example to those you lead?

Prayer: Lord Jesus, help me by Your power to communicate that I belong to You by the way I act and treat others. I want to please and honor You in everything I do.

DAY 5

"I the Lord search the heart and examine the mind, to reward a man according to his conduct, according to what his deeds deserve" (Jer. 17:10).

We are rewarded by the fruit of our doings when our intentions are tried by God. Even when our behavior and deeds are "good," the Lord judges by the stricter standard of His will. We are to fulfill His plans for our lives. Good actions when self-generated rather than God- inspired are worthless and fruitless.

The care to be taken is not in the doing of the deeds, but in the motive behind them. Are we seeking to be righteous before men or before God? Are our deeds God-ordained? The Father rewards us accordingly.

Is the fruit of your deeds going to reap a reward? Have you examined your heart lately?

Prayer: Heavenly Father, help me to be aware of my behavior at all times that I may reflect Your standards.

DAY 6

"Then a cloud appeared and enveloped them, and a voice came from the cloud: 'This is my Son, whom I love. Listen to him!'" (Mark 9:7).

During that remarkable event, the transfiguration of Christ, the Father spoke directly to Peter, James, and John. "This is my beloved Son. You listen to Him!" Pointed words of advice from a loving Father. "Pay attention—hear Him."

Leading God's people requires a listening ear, one that hears and responds to Christ's instructions. Often in communication we are better talkers than listeners. But we'd be wise to heed this command from the Father, "Constantly listen and obey My Son. I love Him." If we hear the Son, we hear the Father.

Are you listening? Can you hear God? Have you given Him your ears—and your heart?

Prayer: Heavenly Father, grant that I will have ears to hear Your message and the heart to obey.

DAY 7

"My dear brothers, take note of this: Everyone should be quick to listen, slow to speak and slow to become angry" (Jas. 1:19).

A fool's voice comes with many words, but a wise man draws near to God to listen and obey. I like the reminder that God is in heaven, and we are on earth. He has a better perspective on things!

James' wise warning is for those of us who are often slow to listen, quick to speak and easily angered. Instead we should hold our tongue and listen. To those who hear us, an unbridled tongue may cause them to question our testimony and even to question its validity.

Are you a listener or a talker? Do you control your anger and your tongue?

Prayer: Lord Jesus, too often I talk instead of listening. Help me to be more sensitive to those who look to me for guidance and adjust my actions accordingly.

FOR FURTHER REFLECTION

1. As transmitters of the message of Jesus Christ, every word spoken and action taken reflects our message. Jesus tells us, "For out of the overflow of the heart the mouth speaks" (Matt. 12:34). What does your speech communicate to those around you?

a. Read the following verses and write phrases which give further insight.

> 1 Peter 4:11; Psalm 15; 37:30-31; Proverbs 8:7-8; 31:26

b. What instructions do you find in the following verses for speech?

> Colossians 4:6; Ephesians 4:29; 5:4; Matthew 12:36

2. What do you find most difficult in communicating?

3. List three practical ways you can overcome this difficulty. Pray for God's wisdom for better communication and ask for healing in your relationship with anyone you have offended through poor communication.

[Frank Damazio in The Making of a Leader contrasts the qualities of a poor and good listener—ed.]

The Poor Listener:
Tunes out subjects he finds uninteresting or boring.
The Good Listener:
Searches for information to acquire additional insights to help.
The Poor Listener:
Judges the speaker by outward appearance/manner.
The Good Listener:
Judges by content rather than speaker/manner.
The Poor Listener:
Is overstimulated by one thought, unable to concentrate on rest of speech.
The Good Listener:
Withholds emotional reactions until he comprehends whole idea.
The Poor Listener:
Uses only one style note taking at all times.
The Good Listener:
Flexible in note taking, adapting to each speaker.
The Poor Listener
Expends little or no listening energy or concentration.
The Good Listener:
Expends much listening energy on communicator.
The Poor Listener:
Avoids new challenges and does not appreciate unfamiliar areas of speech.
The Good Listener
Minimizes and ignores possible distractions.
The Poor Listener:
Operates with closed mind, allows emotional words to interfere with careful evaluation.
The Good Listener
Listens to all material in its variety, attempts to see some significance.[5]

NOTES

[1]Max DePree, *Leadership Is an Art* (New York: Bantam, Doubleday, Dell, 1989), 69.

[2]William Bachus, *Telling Each Other the Truth* (Minneapolis, Minn: Bethany House Publishers, 1985), 139.

[3]Corrie ten Boom, *Clippings from My Notebook* (World Wide Publishing, 1984), 56.

[4]Annie Chapman, "Love Was Spoken," copyright.

[5]Frank Damazio, *The Making of a Leader* (Portland: Bible Temple Publishing, 1988), 228.

Understanding and implementing important aspects of leadership prepares us to create a team atmosphere among those we lead. By living out the character qualities described in this book, the leader becomes a person in whom followers can place their trust. This trust provides a security in the leader/follower relationship which allows the follower to take down her protective guard, risk being known, and consider entering into an in-depth communication with other people on the team.

An effective leader values every "team-player." She seeks from each member contribution to the decision-making process as well as assistance in the implementation of proposed actions. Every member needs to participate in order for each project to succeed and each organizational group to function at peak efficiency.

Max DePree writes, "Momentum comes from a clear vision of what the corporation ought to be, from a well-thought-out strategy to achieve that vision, and from carefully conceived and communicated direction and plans that enable everyone to participate and be publicly accountable in achieving those plans." Participation management, or the "inclusive" method of leadership was Jesus' method with His disciples. He said, "I no longer call you servants, because a servant does not know his master's business. Instead, I have called you friends, for everything that I learned from my Father I have made known to you" (John 15:15).

In building relationships with those you lead, the extra time spent attempting to prayerfully create a team mind-set is worth the effort. Implementing teamwork follows God's design as seen both in Christ's leadership and the function of Christ's body. God will honor your desire to see every individual develop her fullest potential for His greatest glory. Consider new ways you can enhance your leadership through a team ministry concept.

—L. R. M.

CHAPTER 12

CREATING A TEAMWORK MIND-SET

Linda McGinn

Linda R. McGinn is the author of *Growing Closer to God, Resource Guide for Women's Ministries, The Bible Answers Questions Children Ask,* and the Bible study series *Women in the Word.* Ms. McGinn is a graduate of Gordon College, Wenham, Massachusetts, with a B.A. in biblical and theological studies. She and her husband Samuel are parents to Ruth, John, and Sarah.

As the committee members gathered, I scanned the walnut-paneled shelves. A musty odor permeated the small library of age-cherished books. I gently slipped my finger over the rough, dried leather binding of one. The book-lined wall seemed to embrace the seven women seated around the oval table. Having flown to Atlanta for this important meeting, we each represented one of the six geographic areas of the nation. Our purpose was to discuss and determine the direction for women's ministry in our denomination.

Anticipation heightened as the coordinator distributed crisp, royal blue folders. "As the Women's Advisory Sub-Committee," Susan explained, "I see your role as crucial to my work as coordinator. You each represent women from different geographic cultures, attitudes, ideas, and needs. I'm dependent on the wisdom and insight God gives you to make decisions critical to our ministry's future. Teamwork will be the foundation of the committee."

IMPERATIVE NATURE OF TEAMWORK

Through this committee's labor and my involvement in many similar organizations, I have come to recognize another imperative aspect of leadership—teamwork. To understand the importance of Christian teamwork, we need only to look to Jesus and

His ministry. When He began His ministry, He didn't assume that He would do it alone. He immediately began to look for suitable companions to teach and send forth.

First, He was careful in His selection. He chose men with diversified interests and backgrounds—fishermen, tax collector, and businessmen—and appreciated their particular qualities. He knew they would be carrying His message to every type of person, in all walks of life.

Before He sent them out into the world, He trained them so that all would be preaching the same message, the good news of His Father's love. As a team they traveled together, observing, praying, talking, learning, being prepared.

Jesus valued each disciple, looking upon them as individuals. He spent time with each one, as well as with the group. We read, "Jesus withdrew with his disciples to the lake" (Mark 3:7), and realize how often He shared the personal, intimate details of His future plan with His disciples, details that no one else heard or knew.

We learn from Jesus' example that teamwork most effectively accomplishes any group project. The combination of diverse strengths and experiences creates a stronger whole than the limited resources of one or several working independently.

CREATING A TEAMWORK ATMOSPHERE

How do you create an atmosphere for effective teamwork? We see from Jesus' example the importance of time spent with both individuals and the group, training them through living example and verbal direction.

An effective leader equips each team member with an understanding of the goal and the details of its outworking. Every member has the advantage of the "inside" information, rather than the disadvantage of feeling on the "outside" due to cloistered information clutched by a few. In response to this information new ideas and concerns are welcomed.

In Merrill J. Oster's book, *Vision-Driven Leadership*, he describes the climate necessary for effective teamwork. He writes: "An opportunity climate is an environment in which hierarchy and rigid rules are replaced by team spirit and flexibility. It is an environment that allows people to treat failure as a teacher and to test new ideas without fear of retribution."[1]

Most important is an environment that treats people as the company's main asset and does everything possible to see that people flourish and reach their maximum potential.

To develop this kind of environment, consider the following guidelines:

➤ Care about those who look to you for leadership.
➤ Be open about your future hopes and plans.
➤ Discover the personal goals of others and consider methods of incorporating them with your own.
➤ Be affirmative. Compliment achievement, give verbal pats, and positive reinforcement.
➤ Install and maintain an "open door" policy.

Acceptance is a second important aspect of a healthy teamwork atmosphere. Norma's story describes an often experienced problem concerning acceptance which can unfortunately be found in the Christian community.

Norma had always been a member of a woman's Bible study. When her husband, Wayne, was transferred from the West to East Coast, they moved into a newly developing neighborhood. Most of the residents were transplants like her and anxious to fit into the new community. Soon after moving in, Norma visited other young women in the neighborhood and suggested they start a weekly Bible study group. Starting with six new Christian women, she, being the most qualified, led the study. The young mothers expanded their friendship to include husbands and children. They became a close-knit group of friends.

Three years later the friends met and decided to spearhead a community church, reaching out to other newcomers. Requesting that a seminary student lead them, they met in a local school, and the new church grew quickly. Strangers showed up at the school. A few were mature Christians and well qualified to take leadership roles in the growth of the new congregation.

Norma and her friends wholeheartedly believed the Lord's direction to go out into the world and tell the good news, but they secretly resented the newcomers. They felt that their leadership role was being threatened. "After all," she said to one of her friends, "we are the ones who started all this. Why shouldn't we make the decisions and continue to be the leaders?"

The downfall in Norma's thinking and that of the original team is that of acceptance. The inclusion of more individuals operating in the area of their strengths can do nothing but help the group grow stronger. The burden of the work is lightened and each can specialize more effectively in his or her area of giftedness.

This is exactly God's intent for the body of Christ. He designed His body to be a team, each member indispensable, working together so that His fullest purpose will be realized. We fail to realize that it is to our advantage to encourage the gifts and strengths of every member, welcoming new participants because fresh insight, direction, problem-solving and activity can be introduced. Accepting contributions of others can only help us. With teamwork, and an attitude of acceptance, the expanse of God's creativity can be experienced. God's greatest plans can be performed.

A third essential element in creating a teamwork atmosphere is placing value on the individual. Successful leaders make certain that their followers feel needed and involved. They must feel assured that they are respected as individuals, recognized for their personal strengths and abilities. No one wants to feel that they've been "lost in the crowd."

Jethro, Moses' father-in-law, understood the benefits of teamwork in leadership. He warned that God wouldn't want Moses to become so worn out that he would be unable to handle his other duties. He told him to teach others the decrees and laws and show them how to perform their duties (Ex. 18:17-22). "But select capable men from all the people—men who fear God, trustworthy men who hate dishonest gain—and appoint them as officials over thousands, hundreds, fifties and tens" (v. 21).

By following this kind of advice, leaders are able to offer those under their direction the opportunity to do their best and be their best in order to work and grow.

Relationships are always the most important ingredient in team-building. The leaders' interaction with the group is imperative. The value of relationships always supersedes the completion of the task.

Time spent instilling vision, explaining details, discussing options, and building friendships assures the task a success without making the task the unrelentlessly supreme focus. People are always more important than projects. Even though Jesus' mission was divine, He valued each person as He moved unswervingly toward His goal.

GUIDELINES FOR TEAMWORK

How do we assure that your team will work, that everyone will do her job joyfully and efficiently? First, remember that effective methods help each person on a team discover her personal God-given gifts, talents, and abilities. Each member should be convinced of these attributes and willing to use them for the benefit of all. A leader, on the other hand, should seek the Lord's direction in her choice of workers and jobs, recognizing her own limitations and realizing that each helper has an essential job to perform. Paul reinforces this by writing, "But God has combined the members of the body and has given greater honor to the parts that lacked it, so that there should be no division in the body, but that its parts should have equal concern for each other" (1 Cor. 12:24-25).

By asking the Holy Spirit's guidance in making management decisions, a woman leader can help her helpers grow in their life and work. Through her own experience she can assure them that:

➤ It's more important to be faithful and that success is fleeting.
➤ It's important to reach one's potential, as Christ designed.
➤ It's important to be open to the opinions and desires of others.
➤ Being part of a team involves risk and that it is worth it in order to grow and to reach personal goals.
➤ Being part of a team involves intimacy and that she will be personally accountable to others on the team, as they will be to her.

"INTERNAL MOTIVATION" PROMOTES TEAMWORK

There are many ways of motivating people to do something you wish them to do. During the Industrial Revolution in this country, people were hired on a "piece work" basis. The more work they turned out, the more pay they received. Highly motivated employees turned out more and more until the required daily output increased constantly. Those who were slower or less motivated often were unable to feed their families on the wages they were able to earn.

Other motivational methods used by secular leadership included threats, humiliation, and anger. When all of these failed, manipulation became the next method. By cheering the successful performer with applause, plaques, public commendation, it was thought, everyone would be motivated to do a better job.

Now we know that people are "turned on" most successfully when their motivation is internal. The most common internal need is to be loved. Some contemporary leaders feel that a caring, sympathetic, empathetic attitude is the most successful way to motivate others. A Christian leader will succeed if she convinces her followers that God and she, herself, recognize and honor the person's strengths and abilities and that each worker has something of value to offer others.

Finally, as J. Robert Clinton writes, "Leaders must develop a ministry philosophy that simultaneously honors biblical leadership values, embraces the challenge of the times in which they live, and fits their unique gifts and personal development if they expect to be productive over a whole lifetime."[2]

As we each seek God's daily direction, pray by the Holy Spirit's power to exemplify the character of Christ, and stimulate those we lead to experience God's fullest potential for their lives. Through this we will know the fulfillment of Christ-honoring leadership, the leadership that advances Christ's kingdom and brings glory to God.

THOUGHTS FOR DAILY MEDITATION

"May the grace of the Lord Jesus Christ, and the love of God, and the fellowship of the Holy Spirit be with you all" (2 Cor. 13:14).

Three persons in one—the Father, Son, and Holy Spirit. The Godhead is the supreme example of teamwork. Each person within the team has an important and distinct ministry. Jesus dispenses grace, the Father gives His love, and the Holy Spirit provides fellowship. Their separate roles remind us that the mystery of the Trinity is known to be true through our Christian experience. Each believer experiences first-hand the grace, love, and fellowship coming to her from the Lord. The

Father, Son, and Holy Spirit work together as one and are one, always supporting and complementing one another. Through His combined effort God has saved man from sin and self.

DAY 1

"Members of God's household, built on the foundation of the apostles and prophets, with Christ Jesus himself as the chief cornerstone. In him the whole building is joined together and rises to become a holy temple in the Lord" (Eph. 2:19-21).

The apostles and prophets together laid the foundation of faith as they taught and preached God's Word. Jesus is the essential stone of that groundwork. His church, that is all believers bound together as one, becomes a sacred sanctuary where He dwells.

All believers are God's coworkers. When we are in right relationship with Him through Jesus, we join His team to promote His kingdom. Paul tells us that each of us has an important assignment given to us according to the grace of God. Paul skillfully laid the foundation of faith; others built upon it. But it takes all of God's team united to complete it.

Are you prayerfully working to create a team dedicated to Jesus Christ? Is God the foundation of all your leadership?

Prayer: Father, help me to appreciate each person You have placed under my leadership. Guide me to be sensitive to Your Holy Spirit's will in developing each of us to work together for Your glory.

DAY 2

"There are different kinds of gifts, but the same Spirit. There are different kinds of service, but the same Lord. There are different kinds of working, but the same God works all of them in all men. Now to each one the manifestation of the Spirit is given for the common good" (1 Cor. 12:4-7).

Here again we see the Trinity at work making believers a team to serve the Lord through His church. Varieties of gifts, service, and accomplishments fulfill His purpose, which is to work for the common good of all believers. Though the gifts and workings differ, God is the same.

Do you encourage those you lead to realize God's higher purposes for their labor? Is God's glory your instant concern?

Prayer: Father, cause me to constantly seek Your purpose above all else. Help me to lead those whom I serve to see Your divine perspective in all they do.

DAY 3

"Then the Lord said to Moses, 'See I have chosen Bezalel, . . . and I have filled him with the Spirit of God, with skill, ability and knowledge in all kinds of crafts . . . Moreover, I have appointed Oholiab, . . . to help him. Also, I have given skill to all the craftsmen to make everything I have commanded you'" (Ex. 31:1-6).

The Lord had a great plan and assignment for the Israelites. They were to make the tent of meeting, the ark of the testimony, and all the other furnishings, just as He commanded. He appointed each man to his task and equipped him by the Spirit with the ability to do his job. Some were goldsmiths and silversmiths, others worked with wood, and some were aides and organizers. This sacred endeavor required teamwork and the supernatural gifts of the Spirit given to each one.

Do you recognize the fitting together of team members is a special working of the Spirit? How do you fit in the team where God has placed you?

Prayer: Lord, thank You for gifting me to be part of Your team in Your body. Help me to work joyfully with others in our sacred duties. May my highest aim be to bring You glory.

DAY 4

"James, Peter and John, those reputed to be pillars, gave me and Barnabas the right hand of fellowship when they recognized the grace given to me. They agreed that we should go to the Gentiles, and they to the Jews" (Gal. 2:9).

The work of the early church fathers exemplified team work and mutual support. God entrusted to each man a task and then motivated and fitted him for it. Acknowledging and supporting each other's unique ministries was important to promoting their common cause. Paul and Barnabas were called to preach mainly to the Gentiles and James and Peter to the Jews. But both recognized God's grace at work in each one of them to accomplish His plan.

Humility is the essence of Christian unity and teamwork. It is the mind-set of a person who has a right attitude toward herself. She recognizes her own worth in the Lord and sees others as deserving preferential treatment. Selfishness and arrogance are enemies to team harmony. Instead we are able to esteem our coworkers, knowing that God will look out for our interests as we look out for others.

Do you acknowledge God's grace in other ministries different from your own? Do you offer support to those who do them?

Prayer: Father, help me to be a supportive member of your body, not only in my own work but in the work of others.

DAY 5

"And Ruth the Moabitess said to Naomi, 'Let me go to the fields and pick up the leftover grain behind anyone in whose eyes I find favor'" (Ruth 2:2).

For love's sake, Ruth willingly left her homeland to stay with her mother-in-law. Together they went back to Bethlehem and established a new life. With humility and trust Ruth worked in Boaz's fields to provide for Naomi. Because of her faithfulness the Lord honored and blessed her efforts. Through her marriage, Ruth, a Gentile, became a direct ancestor of Jesus Christ.

At what cost are you willing to serve others? How has the Lord honored your efforts?

Prayer: Lord, grant me the gift of humility so that I will serve others with support and encouragement without expecting praise.

DAY 6

"When Priscilla and Aquila heard him [Apollos], they invited him to their home and explained to him the way of God more adequately" (Acts 18:26).

This dynamic couple served the church with great zeal. Faithful friends of Paul, they sailed to Syria with him to preach the gospel. There they met Apollos. Recognizing his potential in the Lord, they offered him hospitality as a way to instruct him in the truth of Christ. Priscilla and Aquila helped start the church at Corinth and supported themselves by tentmaking. They opened their home for meetings and gave gladly to the service of the Lord and His people.

Have you committed yourself to the work God has called you to perform? Do you serve your Lord and His people wholeheartedly?

Prayer: Father, may the zeal seen in the lives of these two early Christians be evident in mine, too.

Day 7

"To prepare God's people for works of service, so that the body of Christ may be built up until we all reach unity in the faith and in the knowledge of the Son of God and become mature, attaining to the whole measure of the fullness of Christ" (Eph. 4:12-13).

As each member does her work, the body of Christ builds itself up in love. Our maturity and unity in the faith are the profitable and desired results. Christian teamwork is the means God uses to produce unity. No part of a healthy body can act independently and still nourish its own growth. Each one must work together for the common good. Wholeness makes us complete in Him and is God's intention for His body. Living in truth as we work as a team assures our success.

The oneness of believers validates the mission of Christ to outsiders. Christ gave His honor to us to enable that oneness. Our unity in turn allows the world to recognize the Father and His love. Working as a team bonded in love for this common cause proves Christ's divinity to non-believers, for true oneness only comes from God.

Does your team's oneness show the reality of God to those who don't know Him? Is unity in the faith one of your priorities as a leader?

FOR FURTHER REFLECTION

1. Read 1 Corinthians 12:12-27. In one sentence of twenty-five words or less explain how Christ's body exemplifies a team ministry concept.

a. List three specific actions you can take to create a team atmosphere among those you lead at home, church, work, or any other environment where your leadership is felt.

b. List possible hindrances to creating a teamwork or participation environment. Example: judgmental attitudes among followers

2. Prayerfully consider ways to overcome each of the hindrances above. Cite biblical references which give instruction for overcoming these obstacles. Example: judgmental attitudes—Romans 2:1-4; 14:13

3. Prayerfully ask God to increase Your trust in Him. May you rest in His sovereign control in your leadership situations. Ask for His ability to "let go" of the personal control and trust in the involvement of others to plan and complete each task. Trust that He is able to work everything in a way that accomplishes His perfect will.

NOTES

[1]Merrill J. Oster, *Vision-Driven Leadership* (San Bernardino, Calif.: Here's Life Publishers, 1991), 82-83.

[2]J. Robert Clinton, *Making of a Leader* (Colorado Springs, Colo.: NavPress, 1988), 180.

AFTERWORD

In this book, successful Christian women leaders have discussed God-dependent actions, decisions, and personal strengths that have been the basis for their successes. It is my hope you will use their words as a road map, assisting you to lead the people God has placed in your path.

As you evaluate the leadership resources in this book, the following summary suggests practical tips to help you demonstrate effective, consistent leadership.

QUALIFYING AS A LEADER

Do you think of yourself as a leader? Do you agree that Christians need to be leaders as they work to change the current direction of the world? When you examine yourself, you will find that you have one or more of the leadership qualities that are mentioned in this book. Activating these God-given qualities is the challenge of leadership. As you, like Moses, acknowledge your inability and rely on God's abundant provision, you become God's leader and there are no limits to your effectiveness in fulfilling His purposes. Here are some additional tips to help you get started.

Good leaders have an organized plan. Before you face those you are to lead, you should have a blueprint of the action to be taken. A good leader first prays and asks God for an initial plan so that she leads according to His directions. Goals to reach, tasks to be completed, assignments to be made—all these are considered before the first meeting. Yet, she is not tied to her plan. She encourages suggestions and gives thoughtful consideration to others' ideas.

Good leaders take risks. When God told Abraham to pack up all of his belongings and head for a new and unknown land, Abraham didn't hesitate. We often stress Abraham's faith, but we should note that he risked everything for God. Mary, too, risked ridicule and rejection to follow God's plan for her life. Young, afraid, and unprepared, she said, "Yes, Lord," when she was asked to do one of the most difficult things a girl then could imagine—have a seemingly illegitimate child.

Today, God's leaders are asked to take risks, to reach out to people they neither know nor understand, and to lead even when their leadership is being questioned. But with God's grace and help, they, like Abraham and Mary, move on in faith.

Good leaders recognize the worth of others. Often leaders find it difficult to recognize that others are doing a good job. They are reluctant to share the credit, or they fear that their leadership will be threatened. With a vision for the complete project and an encouraging attitude, an able Christian leader is open to recognize the worth of others and is sincere in recognizing their efforts.

Good leaders are role models. Being sensitive to others and desiring to serve as a representative of Christ are major qualities of a leader for Christ. Usually when you smile at a person, she'll return the smile. Being a leader is much like that. Your willingness to meditate on God's Word and spend time in intimate fellowship with Jesus, desiring to fulfill His will in all you do, will be reflected in your countenance and actions. Through you, others will see Jesus and desire to be like Him, following your leadership as they pursue Him.

Good leaders are enthusiastic. To lead successfully, a Christian woman is excited about the good news and shows it. She wants to share it with others, showing the love of Christ. Who wants to follow a frowning, sharp-tongued leader? Not many. You can imagine Mary's excitement when she heard that Jesus was no longer in the tomb. He had risen. She was so thrilled she raced into the city to tell the apostles. This is the kind of excitement we feel when we think about His gospel and have the opportunity to lead others to go out and tell about it.

Good leaders turn to God for guidance. People who lead are often reluctant to ask for help. They may consider it a sign of weakness. As you ask yourself if you are qualified to lead, remember that only God is qualified and He, by His Holy Spirit, enables you. In yourself, you are weak. He will strengthen you and help you develop in areas where you are weak.

Remember these qualities when you are asked to take a leadership role. First ask God to reveal the personal talents and gifts with which He has equipped you. God has graciously given each one of us special talents and attributes. As one of His children, these qualities are yours, but are only activated as you draw upon the Holy Spirit's power in every leadership situation, whether in a secular or Christian environment. Just as Jesus prepared His disciples to represent Him throughout the known world, He prepares you with His Word and His perfect example to reach your world for Him.

Paul writes, "Do not think of yourself more highly than you ought, but rather think of yourself with sober judgment, in accordance with the measure of faith God has given you. Just as each of us has one body with many members, and these members do not all have the same function, so in Christ we who are many form one body, and each member belongs to all the others. We have different gifts, according to the grace given us" (Rom. 12:3-6).

Seek to know Him so well that His character qualities become yours. Desire above all else to be His reflection. Then ask Him to use you effectively so that the project or activity will be a shining light to the world for Him.

Consider the thoughts and suggestions described by these successful Christian women leaders. Remember, you may not have all the leadership qualities mentioned in this book, but God does. In you He can develop any quality He desires and enable you to become His representative to the world. So, I pray that through the experiences and understandings of the Christian women represented here, you will become an effective and loving Christian leader.